THE PLAN, THE THOUGHT, THE PURPOSE
a Christian novel by Carrie E. Robinson
(Jeremiah 29:11)
Edited by Claire L. Maset

(c) 2014 by Carrie E. Robinson

Published by Carrie E. Robinson

Printed in the United States of America by Createspace

All Rights Reserved.

Library of Congress Cataloging-in-Publication Data

The Plan, The Thought, The Purpose - July 9, 2014

ISBN -13:978 - 0692244401 (Carrie E. Robinson)

ISBN- 10:0692244409

DEDICATIONS

To my Lord Jesus Christ

"How precious are Your thoughts towards me, thoughts of peace, hope and a future." I am eternally grateful and Yours.

To My Husband, Merrill

for revealing to me my inner strength daily and loving me unconditionally.

"I love you for eternity"

To My Children, Juella, Peppur and Jodis

for your constant challenges that taught me to pray without ceasing. I am so proud to be your mother and I Love You ALL.

To my immediate family, The Dunham's and The Herrings, ALL of my siblings, aunts, uncles, cousins, nieces, nephews, in-laws, grandchildren and God-sons

for the purpose you each played in helping me discover the plan God has for me. Thank you and I'm forever grateful.

To my friends, Evangelist Veronica Rawls, Prophetess Shirley Henderson, Apostle Clara Lawrence, Author Leslie Haskins, Lady Joyce Williams, Michele Henderson-Wilson, Barbara Celeste Bailey, Evang. Maggie O. McAllister, Paralegal Louise Cook, Jackie Brown and my babysis Jacquie Dunham

for believing in me and for your continued love, support and prayers. Each of you are treasured and priceless gems.

To My Editor, Neighbor and Friend, Claire L. Maset

for your candidness, diligence and sacrifices you made to complete this novel. Thanks for your spirit of excellence.

#LOVETHYNEIGHBOR

To Vicky Anderson
Thanks so much for
your support.
There's purpose in the pain we
experience in life, but know that's
it's all A part of God's plan to bring us
into our greatness!!

CL Robinson   11/23/2014

iii

CELEBRATING THE MEMORIES, THE PLAN, THE

THOUGHT, THE PURPOSE AND THE BELOVED LIVES

OF

MY GRANDMOTHER DAISY J. HERRING-WALKER

MY FATHER JIMMY DUNHAM

MY MOTHER MARY L. DUNHAM

MY BROTHER ARTIS C. DUNHAM

MY SISTER MARY E. DUNHAM-BUIE

MY SISTER DOROTHY E. DUNHAM-DARRISON

MY NEPHEW CHARLES L. DUNHAM, SR

MY NEPHEW ANTWAN DUNHAM

DEACON HENRY RAWLS

FIREMAN RONNIE L. HENDERSON 9/11/2001

MY FATHER-IN-LAW MERRILL E. ROBINSON, SR

MY MOTHER-IN-LAW IDA MAE PERRY-ROBINSON

MY SISTER-IN-LAW MARILYN "PUDDY" ROBINSON

MY SISTER-IN-LAW RENEE "BO-PEEP" ROBINSON

MY SISTER-IN-LAW JUANITA HAYES-DUNHAM

MY BROTHER-IN-LAW ROBERT J.WINFIELD, JR.

MY BROTHER-IN-LAW LEROY DARRISON

INTRODUCTION

Life is an amazing journey with many *highs* and *lows* orchestrated by God. It is at our *lows* when we are taught even though we often do not realize the lessons until that episode of the *lows* is over. The devastating *lows* I personally experienced, took me to a place of searching and seeking God for answers. These *lows* were extremely painful and almost unbearable.

I know what it feels like to have your heart ripped out because of the pain of deception and lies, betrayal and rejection but by the grace of God I survived and I am still alive...broken and scarred; and altered forever. My horrific *lows* made me stronger, wiser and better. I learned that God loves me and would never intentionally hurt me. In my quest to understand, I found in God's word, Jeremiah 29:11 (KJV). "For I know the plan and thoughts that I think toward you saith the Lord, thoughts of peace and not evil, to give you that expected end." Another version (NIV) says,... "to give you a hope and a future."

Both versions reminds us that God is Omniscient (all- knowing). It is God who has outlined the plan for our lives including the good, the bad and the ugly events of life. I learned to trust Him and not worry about anything. The *highs* teach us the celebratory moments of victory and joy. The *lows* teach us humility and draw us to God for comfort, for peace, for answers. Sometimes, the *lows* can cause so much pain that our limited and self righteous mindset begins to blame God because we lack understanding of the plan.

To this...God says, *I know your name and I know your pain. I hurt when you hurt. I am with you always and I have not forgotten you. I am making you. There is purpose in your pain. Draw closer to Me, don't reject Me*

v

and rebel. I am building your character for the reason you exist.

All of our *highs* and *lows* in life will help us to empathize with the pain we see in others and to genuinely understand their hurt and to know how to effectively pray for them and their needs. The plan that God has for us causes a chain of events to unfold. If that particular thing does not occur, then that subsequent thing would not have happened and you will not learn that lesson.

For example: You overslept and missed the bus and later discovered it crashed. It's just like that... It was a part of God's divine plan for you to over sleep and miss the bus or just the opposite could have occurred. Your unpleasant incident could be for someone else's benefit.

Romans 8:28 declares "ALL things work together for the good to those that love the Lord and are the called according to God's purpose." I pray that this book will take you to that place of acquiescence and confidence in God to know that He is too wise to make any mistakes with your life - TRUST HIM. HE HAS THE ULTIMATE PLAN.

TO THE READER

Is it a figment of our imagination that we are in control of our destiny? This book, THE PLAN, THE THOUGHT, THE PURPOSE reveals in a realistic way, that every detail of our lives is orchestrated by our Creator; right down to the people who come and go in our lives, including the good, the bad, and the ugly. Although this book is about the plight of certain characters, it is also about the Miracle Working Power of God, and His Gifts that he has so graciously given to us, as well as the Power of Prayer.

The names in this book are fictional, but the drama and the Gifts of God that are manifested can be very real. For the believer, skeptics, non believers, and those who are yet undecided, I would like to encourage you to read about the Gifts of God in 1st Corinthians chapters 12 and 14. The manifestation of the Spirit is given for the common good. To one there is given by the Spirit the Word of Wisdom, to another the Word of Knowledge, to another the Gifts of Healing, to another Miraculous Powers, Prophecy, Discerning of spirits, Divers (many) Tongues, and the Interpretation of Tongues. All of these are the works of one and the same Spirit and He distributes them to each one just as He determines.

Perhaps you will recognize the gifts operating in some of the characters in this book. May I boldly add, if these gifts are not operating in you or your church, that does not mean they do not exist. Just as you may not believe in God, doesn't mean He doesn't exist. May I suggest to you that you allow yourself to be vulnerable to the thing of God. Ask for the manifestation to be evident in your life as they are in this book.

Remember, the characters are fictional, but the Miracle Working Power of God is very real and He can meet you right here in this book. There is nothing too hard for God. Our finite mind can't comprehend the infinite mind of God. He knows the plan for our lives from the beginning to the end. It is inevitable and permissible only by God to fulfill the plan, the thought, and purpose of His design. You are his designed masterpiece and I believe it has been ordained by God that you read this book. I pray that this book will encourage you, challenge you, and bless you in Jesus Name.

PROLOGUE

Nate Bishop had been down one man in the maintenance department at Paradise Pillows Manufacturing Company for several months. Nate was in dire need of a highly motivated person who was a hard worker and a self-starter. The ad ran in the Daily Harlem News for three days. Although several had applied for the position, only one stood out in his mind at the end of the third day, Ricky Clay, a well dressed, articulate, soft spoken individual who was seemingly a perfect fit. Since the company was hurting financially, Nate decided not to do the background check as he had always done, which exposed everyone to dangerous and life threatening situations.

Ricky was a calculating and shrewd business man with a charismatic personality who often deceived even the closest of his associates and acquaintances. Ricky was quite appealing to the opposite sex and definitely had confidence like none other. He quickly gained the trust, love and respect of all personnel at Paradise Pillows. Ms. Joni King was an exception. She was a born-again, spirit filled woman with many gifts who came to know God through the painful ordeal of her husband's tragic death.

Teresa Hayward, Nate's assistant, met Ricky Clay in high school ten years earlier. She often thought of Ricky as her future husband. That was until three days ago, when Teresa was not feeling well and left her work station to go to the ladies room. As she approached the room, she heard loud voices coming from Nate Bishop's office. As she peered into the office, she saw Ricky with a gun pressed against Nate's head. Tremendous pain and fear was etched on Nate's face as he nodded his head and collapsed to the floor. Did Ricky shoot him? Panic stricken with no place

I

to run, and hoping she was not seen, Teresa slipped quickly back to her work station. What was she to do now? Suddenly, heavy footsteps were coming toward her. The series of events that happen next will shatter and alter the course of her life forever.

Chapter 1

The soulful voice of Bill Withers rang out, "Lean on me, when you're not strong and I will be your friend, I'll help you carry on...." echoed in Teresa's mind. She had no one to lean on. Feeling rejected and broken, facing the world alone as a single mother, Teresa's job was her only sense of security and stability. It was just enough to pay her bills and take a vacation once a year with Jamie, her eight year old son. Her fiancée, Michael Harden, had dumped her eight years ago, four months after giving birth to their little man, Jamie. Teresa would never forget that evening. Several more songs played on the radio that evening which seemed to foretell the painful break up that was coming. Thelma Houston sang "Don't leave me this way..." followed by "How can you mend this broken heart..." by the Bee Gees played in the background as she cleaned up dinner and made formula and cereal for Jamie to take to Momma King, the babysitter, the next day. Mike came home later than usual for the umpteenth time since Jamie was born, and instead of using his key to let himself in, he rang the doorbell.

"Who is it?" she asked, puzzled as to who it could be at 9 PM. She had expected Mike three hours earlier, and knew he always used his key.

"It's me, Mike."

Teresa opened the door and questioned him, "What happened to your keys?" Mike, smelling heavily of cheap perfume and stale beer, drunkenly stated, "I uh lost them," avoiding eye contact.

"You lost your key to the house, so how did you get home? Where is the car? Both keys were on your key ring, right?" Teresa quizzed angrily without waiting for Mike to answer. "I know there is another woman. I have noticed how you lost interest in me after Jamie was born. I tried to look away and hoped that you would come to your senses, but it is obvious that you have not. So, I am going to help you make a decision! It is me or her? And I want an answer now!" glaring with such disgust.

"Okay, you are right! There is another woman who does not have any children and she does not want any!" he screamed back.

Teresa knew Mike did not want children, and she did not deliberately plan to get pregnant. However, when she found out she was pregnant with his child, she was elated. But Mike wanted her to abort. She was devastated and vowed within her heart...never! Although, being reared by a religious grandma, Teresa sometimes prayed and believed in God but never had an intimate relationship with Him. She knew in her heart that abortions were wrong and no matter what, she would never do such a thing.

Teresa, while in deep thought, was snapped back to reality when she heard Mike say, "I am leaving. I told you I was not ready for the responsibility of raising a child. It was nice when it was just the two of us, you know..."

Teresa interrupted, "His name is Jamie! Mike, he is not just a child. He is your son. His name is Jamie! Jamie Hayward!" Surrendering to the pain in her heart, the tears suddenly flooded her eyes and rolled down her cheeks. She did not notice Mike had walked out the door until it slammed... loud and hard, causing her to jump.

Eight years later, Teresa still struggled with being rejected. She recalled the first day Ricky Clay reported to work at Paradise Pillows. It was then, she decided her past would no longer hold her captive to rejection and loneliness. Ricky's charismatic personality changed everything. Nate Bishop, the owner of Paradise Pillows, had called a meeting to introduce the new employee to his staff. Teresa was focused on finishing up the embroidery on the lace pillow case and was the last to arrive. Just as Nate was asking if anyone had seen Teresa, she opened the door, dressed in black leggings which showed her long slender legs and her shapely figure. Teresa's close cut curly hair framed her face perfectly, accentuating her large brown eyes and small but full lips. A soft coral linen blouse which showed a hint of cleavage against her soft mocha colored skin seemed to radiate *soft and ladylike.* Her eyes sparkled with new life when Ricky's eyes met hers...and she froze. It seemed like eternity. Everything appeared to be in slow-motion.

Nate broke the spell by clearing his voice and speaking loudly.

"Aahhhh Teresa, will you come in and take a seat please?"

Teresa, hearing the soft laughter of her peers, blushed and quickly took the first empty chair. Fear, embarrassment, excitement and a myriad of emotions would not allow her to look in Ricky's direction. It was extremely hard to stay focused on what Nate was saying.

Teresa had drifted back to the effect he had on her while in high school.

His popularity and charm were the talk of all the girls, and she was no exception. Sometimes she would see him in the halls and in the cafeteria, and he would smile and wink at her, but she was always so bashful she could only turn her eyes away and give him a shy smile.

Because Teresa had always been smitten by his charm, even in high school, she thought perhaps life was giving her another chance when he became employed as a technician in the Maintenance Department. Finally, a man with possibilities that seemed interested in her. It had been a long eight years since Mike had walked out on her and Jamie. Perhaps Ricky could be a good father to Jamie and a great husband to her. She went on a few dates here and there, but nothing remotely serious until now. Was Ricky the answer to her loneliness?

Teresa always remembered what her grandmother told her when she was a little girl. "If you can't put into words what you want to say to God, He always listens to what is unspoken in your heart." Was Ricky the answer from God through her unspoken prayer, when her heart was broken into pieces? Although, Teresa was very pretty, she lacked confidence in herself and often desired to be like other girls who were outgoing and popular.

"That was then, this is now" she reasoned within herself. "I am now a mature woman and..."

Again, Nate suddenly broke her thought by asking her, "How many boxes were on order to ship out?"

Teresa answered immediately hoping she did not appear to be in deep thought.

"Only fifteen so far. They were left over from Friday. Maybe by the end of the week, we can produce thirty five if we have buyers."

The numbers had been very low the past six months and Nate was fearful of the possibility that the shop would close if sales did not increase. Nate felt that if he had a technician in the Maintenance Department, he could spend more time networking and making new contacts who would purchase his pillows and pillow cases. Nate focused back on Ricky and motioned for him to stand as he introduced him as the new technician for the Maintenance Department.

"Please everyone make Ricky feel welcome and return back to work. Let's make that quota..." Everyone smiled and shook hands with Ricky, welcoming him on board.

Teresa still sat...frozen to the chair as people began leaving one by one. Suddenly there he was...smiling.

"So, you don't want me here? You heard the boss. I am waiting for you to welcome me," he teased.

Teresa drew strength from within, refusing to be the shy high school girl. She stood and stared him straight in his eyes and replied, "I stayed to give you a personal welcome," extending her hand, which he graciously took and kissed.

"So very nice to see you again. It has been almost ten years and you are as stunning as you were in high school," he oozed, as she blushed inwardly, pulling her hand back.

"Ahhh, I know you say that to all the ladies," she said smiling, slapping his hand away as she quickly headed for the door.

CHAPTER 2

Slick Rick was his street name. He and his boys called themselves Brothers of the Yoked and Shackled (BOYS). Ricky, Dante, Billy, Henry and Big Red grew up on the Southside of Chicago. They were inseparable and vowed their allegiance to each other forever as young kids. When Ricky's parents divorced, his mother, Maxine moved back to Harlem to be with her parents. Maxi, as she was called, thought the move was an excellent decision because Ricky and his friends were constantly getting into trouble with the law. She was afraid Ricky would be killed like Henry and Big Red.

It happened one night when Henry and Big Red hit the local gas station/convenient market just before closing. They had tied up the owner and left him in the back of the store while they ransacked the store and the cash register. They did not realize that where they left the owner tied and gagged was close enough for him to reach the silent alarm. Just as they had the cash and were leaving, running toward their car, a police car pulled in front of their car blocking them in. Instead of surrendering, they pulled out their weapons and began to fire at the officers. Both Henry and Big Red were killed in the shoot out.

Even though Dante and his family moved to Florida and Billy moved to Texas to live with his uncle after his grandmother passed away, their alliance grew even stronger. Distance could not separate their bond. They spoke three times a day by phone, every day for the next four years, at designated times, no matter what. They trusted no one but each other. Even from a distance, any money gained illegally or otherwise was always shared with the other. They were the *BOYS,* a coalition yoked and shackled forever.

They remained connected, even though Slick Rick lived on the east coast in Harlem, New York, Billy in Texas and Dante in Florida. After the death of Henry and Big Red, they vowed never to do anything without a vote. They would be smart and plan everything very carefully together. Ricky felt responsible because Henry and Big Red did not inform him of their plan. He always felt he was the leader and it would have never happened if he had known. He felt confident that he would have been able to stop their plan to rob the store. It was a deep loss to Slick Rick and the *BOYS.*

CHAPTER 3

Being employed by Paradise Pillow was a perfect set-up for Ricky and the *BOYS*. Ricky had just gotten off the phone with Dante, and was now waiting to hear from Billy. The first shipment had arrived about thirty minutes earlier at the Paradise Pillows warehouse and Ricky nervously waited for the next shipment being delivered by Sal.

The unsuspecting driver, Sal Tully, had worked for Paradise Pillows Manufacturing Company for two months. Sal had eagerly taken the job after his wife threw him out because of his infidelity. With no job, no money and no place to go, he slept and lived in his car. Oftentimes Sal looked through the garbage after hours for food. Ricky spotted Sal in the same place, for several days parked in the back near the warehouse when he came to work. Ricky knew a man that despondent and fraught would probably do anything to get money. Ricky needed a driver to pick up the shipment, and with very calculating thoughts, he quickly came up with a way to persuade Nate to hire another driver to distribute more Paradise Pillows throughout the states.

Wasting no time, Ricky was anxious to share his idea with Nate. Ricky knocked lightly on Nate's door. "Yeah, come on in," yelled Nate, as he was preparing a second cup of coffee.

"Aahhhh Ricky, It is always good to see you. What can I do for you this morning?"

Clearing his throat, Ricky put his serious business mind to work.

"Yes, Nate, I have been thinking about this company and ways to improve productivity and how to make a greater profit each year."

Nate was impressed by Ricky's statement and definitely wanted to hear more. Ricky suggested expanding the territories to other states and incorporating other big chain stores to purchase Paradise Pillows in bulk at 25% above wholesale; stores like Welmark, Kaybos, Marshwells and BWright's, Tarket and Geemarts.

"I have already checked on certain stores in Texas and Florida. I can start the shipments right away. The only problem is the need to hire a driver to make the runs across country to the various designated hubs," hinted Ricky.

Amazed at his brilliance and efficiency, Nate immediately advised Ricky to implement his ideas. In fact, he gave Ricky the authority to hire another driver to help with distribution.

"I will be right on it, Nate. And oh, by the way, thank you."

"No," said Nate, "Thank you, Ricky. I am so pleased to have you here at Paradise. You are like the son I never had."

Nate was thinking of offering Ricky a promotion to Director of Sales after he completed two years with the company, which would be occurring in two months. His peers respected him and he had taken great interest in both the Sales Department, Shipping and Receiving Department, as well as the Maintenance Department. Nate thought, "He is certainly deserving of a promotion." After all, Nate was soon turning sixty-five and wanted to pass on some of the responsibilities of running the company. He was relieved that Ricky was a self-starter and ambitious. Ricky's professionalism and work ethic, at the age of twenty-eight, made him appear to be an experienced, mature and savvy businessman. Nate Bishop had a plan for Ricky Clay and

Ricky Clay had a plan for Nate Bishop and his company---Paradise Pillows.

Slick Rick managed to hold back the calculating evil in his mind. He had to be very careful and clever to make sure everyone looked up to him and trusted him. He worked extremely hard the first year, establishing himself with every employee and especially with Teresa and Nate. He gained their trust and confidence. His acceptance and trust at Paradise was key to the international monopoly. This plan was well thought out and the scheme with the *BOYS* would change his life and theirs forever.

Slick Rick was the mastermind. Dante and Billy worked behind the scenes in their respective cities designating drivers to make the drops at specific locations en route to the various stores while distributing the soft and firm Paradise Pillows.

CHAPTER 4

"Hey Ricky! What's up Man?" said Sal, looking at him with great admiration. Sal felt genuinely indebted to Ricky for helping him get a job and changing his bad situation overnight. He was deeply grateful and thought he would definitely make the best of this opportunity. He had not worked in three months since IBM downsized. He spent most of his day searching the Help Wanted Ads looking for work. He tried to help out at home by preparing dinner, washing clothes, and cleaning but Carolyn, his wife of six years, never seemed to notice any of his contributions or efforts. She only complained, and every day seemed to become more and more sarcastic and irate at his presence.

"You haven't found a job yet?" she would ask.

His answer was always the same, "No, not yet. I am looking."

She never listened to him anymore, no more chatting over dinner, no more sexy gestures, no more... nothing! She quickly showered and went to bed. The next morning she left for work without saying goodbye.

Around noon, Margie, their new neighbor who lived down the hall, stopped to ask if Sal could see what was wrong with her air conditioner. Margie's long reddish brown wig framed her face perfectly. Her deep chocolate complexion with long brown eyelashes was stunning as they shaded her piercing hazel eyes. Margie was a brick house (36-24-36) and she knew how to get what she wanted. And today Sal Tully was the target.

"Sure, no problem," as Sal followed her to her apartment. His heart began pounding as she swayed her body provocatively from right to left. Margie paused, turned, and gave a seductive wink at him which made his whole body feel weak. Sal quickly assessed the problem and told Margie she could call the office and the maintenance crew would add the coolant to the air conditioner. Turning to leave her apartment, Margie brushed her body against his. He pretended not to notice, and escaped to his apartment. Once inside, he was not sure if he heard a knock. Sal listened above his radical breathing and the pounding of his heart and yes, there it was again. She had followed him back to his apartment.

Margie knocked softly for the third time. He knew it was her and that she had one thing on her mind. He hesitated to open the door. Feeling down, defeated, broken and disgusted, he decided, "What the heck. Carolyn is at work and not due home until 5 PM." He quickly opened the door, as if it were a magical moment. Mystified by the unknown and forbidden, he succumbed to the seductive power of Margie's touch and the purring in her throat. Neither spoke as they moved quickly, passing the living room, then the kitchen and into his bedroom which he had shared faithfully with Carolyn for the past six years. He felt alive, wanted and needed. It was to be a moment that was short lived.

Carolyn's boss had asked her to work late to finish up a project and in dire need of extra money, she accepted. With Sal not working, Carolyn felt overwhelmed, depressed and frustrated. Bills were mounting daily. Their phone was turned off the day before. Annoyed because she was not able to call Sal to bring her something to eat, she headed home to make a sandwich.

Carolyn heard sounds coming from the bedroom. She cussed and muttered under her breath, "I can't believe he is still in bed watching TV. Why isn't he out looking for a job?" Just as she was about to call out to him, she heard a female giggling. Carolyn was convinced, *that* was *not* on the TV! Rage overtook her body and mind, as she grabbed her grandmother's wooden rolling pin from the kitchen counter.

"Kill him! Kill him!" the voices in her head yelled to her. "Kill him!!"

Carolyn charged into the bedroom swinging the rolling pin with all her might. Immediately, Sal and Margie were scrambling trying to shield themselves and escape Carolyn's wrath and her grandmother's rolling pin.

Sal understood Carolyn's rage when she caught him in bed with Margie. He was really grateful he escaped with only a large 'egg' on the back of his head. And yes, he was grateful for the clothes he managed to grab on the way out which included his keys, but did not include socks and shoes. He had never seen Carolyn in such a fit of rage. He actually feared for both his life and Margie's. While Carolyn focused her wrath on Sal, Margie bolted for the door leaving Sal to fend for himself.

"Whew," Sal sighed, once on the outside. "At least I am safe for now!" He had no food, no money, no socks, no shoes, and an excruciating headache! Sal cried and pleaded with God to please forgive him for what he had done and to please help him.

Slick Rick cautiously approached Sal on the third morning after the incident. He offered him a job as a driver with a week's pay in advance to transport pillows to various hub stations in different states. Sal was sure God heard his prayers. Ricky even gave him a pair of his shoes to get started which was the exact size he needed. Sal looked up to the heavens and smiled at God and thought, "You really heard me, huh?" Grateful for another chance, he vowed he would work hard, save as much money as he could and return home to Carolyn and ask for forgiveness. Perhaps she would be willing to forgive him just as God had.

CHAPTER 5

For the first time in the past two years, Teresa had to stay late to keep up with the demands of the production of Paradise Pillows. She was elated that she was earning extra money to take Jamie on a more extravagant vacation. At last, Teresa felt a sense of belonging, security and love. Since Ricky was introduced into the company nearly two years earlier, they have been inseparable. Ricky was the perfect gentleman. Even when Teresa asked him to move in with her, he told her he respected her too much to live with her and not be her husband. Although they each had their own place to live, Teresa looked forward to their vacations together. It felt like a real family in the true sense. He was caring and loving, a great role model to Jamie, often taking him fishing on Saturdays, while Teresa pampered herself to look good for Ricky. Ricky often patted himself on the back at how good he was at manipulating and deceiving others, even those who were closest to him.

Sales increased over one hundred percent and Nate was ecstatic as he unlocked his office door. It was a Saturday morning and the office was closed, but Nate wanted to embrace the moment of feeling successful again before retiring. Nate began to go over the inventory statement Teresa had left on his desk the night before. All was wonderful. Nate often wondered why he had never thought of establishing hubs throughout the country to expand his business as Ricky had done. Within one year of Ricky managing Paradise Pillow's inventory, the company productivity doubled in sales as well as doubled its clientele.

Nate decided to check on the shipment of pillows that were ready to be shipped. As Nate entered the warehouse, he noticed that it appeared to be reorganized and sectioned off into four separate areas. He was so pleased to see how well Ricky had coordinated things. As he went to inspect the first area, he smiled at how all the boxes with the label *soft and firm* held six pillows in each of the twenty boxes in that area ready for shipping. The same occurred in the second area, labeled *soft* and the third area labeled *firm*. As Nate approached the fourth separated area, he noticed they too were marked *soft and firm* but each of these boxes had the initials *BOYS* under each label. Curious as to what could be in those boxes, Nate moved in closer to inspect the contents. Nate recognized the embroidery that Teresa had done on many of the pillow cases over the years, yet there were no pillows. He saw only the cases which appeared to be lumpy.

In the past, certain high-end clients would order pillows along with a few pillowcases for their inventory like Marcy's and Bloomerdales, but never to this magnitude. Nate lifted one of the pillowcases and immediately knew, due to the weight, that pillows were certainly not in these cases. He lost his balance and fell into the array of boxes causing the concealed smuggled goods to tumble out of several cases. He was shocked to discover that several pillow cases contained bales of marijuana and several cases contained a white powdery substance. Nate assumed it to be cocaine which was stacked and wrapped in clear plastic. Stunned at his findings, Nate felt sick to his stomach and began to hyperventilate.

CHAPTER 6

Ricky gave Sal a head nod and nervously began moving the boxes marked *soft and firm* pillows out of the delivery truck. The pillow boxes labeled *BOYS* contained bales of marijuana and many kilos of cocaine. Ricky moved quickly, eyeing the boxes marked *firm and soft* as he instructed Sal where to unload the boxes in the warehouse. The biggest shipment ever had finally arrived!

Sal had been working steadily now for two months and longed to see Carolyn. He decided this weekend would be the time. He would drive over and surprise her. So ashamed and disgraced by his actions, he had never made any contact with her after he left fleeing for his life. He only thought of ways to prove his repented heart. He had managed to save most of his money except for what he paid for his temporary shelter in an old "drug using, pimps with prostitutes" motel on the other side of town, (which was a huge upgrade from living and sleeping in his car). He was excited to finally be able to contribute and take care of his wife and home again. He spent many hours praying that God would restore his relationship with Carolyn and that she would welcome him back home. He was so ashamed of his apparent act of infidelity and realized Margie had probably seduced many men before. She was skilled...a real professional. She was attractive, sexy, feminine, a real brick house, and she knew it.

Sal had a restless Friday night in anticipation of seeing Carolyn the next day. Saturday morning was beautiful as Sal got into his car to drive across town to the apartment he had once shared with his wife. Sal felt both grateful and guilty, even though he did not commit the act of adultery. He was still guilty of an uncompromising situation. He was so ashamed. Carolyn was a good woman and deserved a lot more respect than he showed her. He thought about how disrespectful his father had been to his mother. He vowed as a young boy, he would always love and respect his wife. "How could this have happened?" he cried. Oh, how he wanted to tell her what a fool he had been.

Carolyn awoke, dreading to face day number fifty five. It had been almost two months since she caught Sal in bed with Margie and even though very hurt, she was lonely and missed Sal. She had not heard from him since that painful day she clobbered him in the head. He was last seen running for his life with no shoes, no money and no socks. She wondered how he was getting along. She had no way of reaching him, no way to find out his whereabouts. She knew that if he wanted to call her, he could not because the phone was still shut off. Every day, when Carolyn would arrive home, she looked for Sal's car in their designated parking space. Every day she had new hope. Carolyn wanted to believe that one day Sal would come home to her, but was far from being convinced this would happen.

Margie felt so guilty for what she had done; but what amazed her, was that she had never felt guilty about seducing men before. Somehow this time was different; "Maybe because I got caught?" she reasoned. She thought surely the feeling would pass. It had been months now and it was still very fresh in her mind; the day Carolyn walked in on her and Sal in their bed. Carolyn's face appeared in her dreams every night, crying, and screaming, "NO, NO, NO... not my Sal!"

Drained and frustrated from lack of sleep, she began to speak out loudly to herself, "Have you no shame? Have you ever thought of the hurt you have caused so many people, and the destruction to so many relationships?" What was happening to her she wondered. Why did this bother her so much, as tears began to swell in her eyes.

This emotional roller coaster was definitely something new. Margie was determined she would get some sleep that night as she started down the stairs to the drug store for an over-the-counter sleeping pill. Margie was always very promiscuous and spoiled by men, but was never satisfied by any of them enough to stay in a committed relationship. There was always something that seemed to be more appealing than the last one she took to her bed, married or single.

CHAPTER 7

Carolyn forced herself to get to the supermarket to pick up a few items before it closed. Sal was greatly missed because he always made sure there were plenty of fresh vegetables and fruit in the refrigerator. Now this was just one of a million things he did that Carolyn missed. Perhaps if she had been more understanding and loving toward him he would have never cheated on her. She knew she had pushed him away. Her heart hurt so badly, but the pain was quickly replaced with anger and revenge, as she suddenly eyed Margie leaving the building. Carolyn parked her car. Margie had no place to go, no place to run and no place to hide. This was the first time she saw Carolyn since she fled from her apartment.

The horrible scene of Margie in her bed with her husband was almost too much to bear. Their eyes met. No escape for either. They must face each other head on. Carolyn's athletic frame moved quickly up the walkway with her eyes locked on Margie. Margie tried to look away, but the anger and pain on Carolyn's face paralyzed her. Within seconds, Carolyn felt a sharp pain in her right arm and fist. Suddenly there was Margie on the pavement with blood pouring profusely from her nose. Margie cried and pleaded, "Please don't hurt me!" Apparently Carolyn's right arm and fist made contact with Margie's nose with such force that it knocked Margie off her feet. Carolyn was outraged, shocked, and thrilled. She felt a sense of satisfaction as well as a sense of embarrassment. She had never had a fight in her life and was still stunned trying to figure out if she had actually punched Margie in the nose and knocked her down.

Margie began to reach for her bag to get some tissues to wipe her bloody nose. Carolyn, fearing she might be reaching for some type of weapon, kicked her bag from within her reach. Carolyn was trying to calm herself and moved backward to get her composure. Margie surrendered to her position on the hard pavement, reluctant to move.

"I deserved that and I am so sorry, but what you think happened, never took place. We had been in bed for only a minute before you came in and hit him in the back of the head with that rolling pin. Had you been a few minutes later, it would have definitely been different. And again, I am so sorry," Margie whined. Carolyn could not believe her ears reiterating what she had just learned. She spoke more to herself than to Margie..."Nothing really happened?"

Margie once again made an effort to get her bag. Carolyn did not move this time, still trying to comprehend what Margie had just told her. Margie managed to retrieve her bag and clean up her bloody nose with some tissue she found deep within the bag.

Carolyn now focused on Margie's disheveled appearance. Her wig was twisted noticeably, blood smeared on her nose and cheek while one of her eyelashes lay abandoned next to her on the pavement. She looked like a hot mess! Carolyn tried hard to suppress the laughter but to no avail. Carolyn began to laugh so hard she started crying. Tears rolled down her cheeks as she looked at Margie. Soon, both ladies were laughing hysterically as Carolyn reached out her hand to help Margie up. Margie gladly accepted, looking around to see if anyone had witnessed this embarrassing altercation. She did not see anyone and continued to laugh hysterically with Carolyn as they made their way back to their own apartments. Margie felt relieved that it was over now and perhaps *now* she could get a good night's sleep.

CHAPTER 8

Nate Bishop, still feeling light-headed, managed to get back to his office, lock it up and make his way to his car. Still in a state of shock, Nate sat motionless for what seemed like hours, trying to decipher what he had just discovered. "Could Ricky be responsible for this?" he wondered. "No, Ricky was so well loved and respected. Could the new hire Sal be responsible? If that were true, then surely Ricky must have known what was going on. No, that is not possible. Ricky could never betray me like that. Could Teresa be involved somehow? They had been inseparable since Ricky became employed. How long has this been going on? Why was I so trusting?" Nate's thoughts raced. He turned the key in the ignition and started for home. He could not tell Lola, his wife of forty-two years, what he had discovered. He always loved her and vowed to take care of and protect her. She was the epitome of a perfect lady and wife, who adored her husband and was very supportive. Although Lola never had much to do with Nate's business, she was very involved with the people who worked for him. She would pay extra attention to make sure their birthdays, anniversary dates, special occasions, and holidays were recognized by inviting the employees and their families to celebrate at their home.

Lola heard Nate's car in the driveway of their modest 3000 square foot two story colonial home that they designed and built the second year after they were married. They planned to have lots of room for the two children they wanted to have and raise there. Unfortunately, that was a short lived dream. Soon after moving into their dream home, Lola suffered female complications and needed to have a hysterectomy. Nate always assured her that as long as he had her, it did not matter. He loved her with all his heart. He suggested if she really wanted to have kids, they could adopt. Lola did not want to consider that option so they never had any children. Nate was fine with that.

Lola watched Nate as he exited the car and closed the door. He appeared to be in a daze. His shoulders drooped and his head hung low as if he were carrying the weight of the world on his shoulders. Lola ran to the door to greet him, knowing something was wrong, but wondering what could it be. The business was doing better than it had been in the last five years and Nate was looking forward to cutting back on his hours and giving more authority and responsibility to Ricky Clay. Nate, hearing her open the door, lifted his head and tried hard to put on his normal smile, not wanting Lola to know of his discovery. Lola knew him all too well. She sensed something was not right and was determined to find out what was wrong over dinner.

It was Saturday evening as Lola and Nate rode in almost silence as they went to dinner at their favorite restaurant, Lil Lady Elite.

"You seem far away tonight Nate. Is everything okay?" Lola asked.

"Oh yes Sweetie. All is well and nothing at all for you to worry about," as he reached over and put his hand over hers.

She held his hand and turned to look at him. Feeling her stare, he stayed focused on the road. She knew he was withholding something and *the something* was big. Lola had never seen him look and act this way since she knew him. "What could it be? Was there another woman? Was he tired of me after all these years?" she pondered.

"No!" she resisted, "Nate loves me. He would never be unfaithful. He is still the perfect gentlemen and very loving in every way."

They had just settled in by the glowing fireplace, a spot where they sat for years and had just ordered their appetizers when Nate turned white as a sheet. Lola gasped and screamed.

"Nate, are you alright?" Nate's body suddenly became rigid as he grabbed his chest and collapsed face down on the table.

"Help! Someone call 911 please!" Lola screamed, as she began to pull Nate from the table to the floor to check his vitals. There was a rapid heartbeat and Nate was sweating and shaking, appearing to be in and out of consciousness. Lola held his head and comforted him until the paramedics arrived, which felt like forever.

CHAPTER 9

Ricky arrived early Saturday morning to pick up Jamie for their usual outing; fishing in the private pond just on the out skirts of town. Teresa had made a nice lunch for them. Ricky looked forward to this time alone with Jamie because he could relax and carefully make his next calculated move. The *BOYS* had everything invested in this deal. This was the biggest shipment yet. Business was growing and there wasn't any room for error. Every detail had to be well thought out, deliberate and precise.

As Ricky and Jamie settled in to fish, Ricky thought of the first time he met Jamie two years earlier. He was a typical six year old, full of questions and followed Ricky everywhere. He beamed with excitement when Ricky would come over and spend time with him and Teresa. Jamie, now age eight, saw Ricky as a father figure in his life. Ricky made sure he shaped Jamie's thinking to know him in that way.

When Jamie turned eight years old, Ricky lavished him with lots of gifts and toys. He convinced Teresa that he wanted to make sure she and Jamie were well taken care of and insisted on opening a bank account in Jamie's name.

It seemed so innocent and natural for a man who loved her and her son to show his love and kindness. In fact she felt overjoyed that Ricky loved her son so much he would even consider doing such a thing for someone who was not his biological son. Teresa trusted Ricky with Jamie and loved them both deeply.

Teresa remembered all to well the day he opened the account. It had been about 2:30 on a Friday afternoon several months prior. Ricky left work early to meet Jamie at 3:00 when he would get off the school bus on the corner near his home. Teresa was still at work when Ricky approached her that he would soon be leaving to meet Jamie to open the bank account in his name but needed Jamie's social security number. Without hesitation, Teresa smiled and looked around to see if anyone was looking. Feeling it was safe, she hungrily kissed him. She teased him and told him there was more to follow as she wrote Jamie's social security number down on a memo pad. Ricky teased her back and smacked her softly on the butt as he turned and took the pad while yelling over his shoulder. "Oh, by the way," he shouted, "If Nate should ask, I left for the day and Jamie and I will meet you later this evening for dinner!"

Ricky arrived in his 1975 black and gold Chevy just as Jamie stepped off the bus. As usual, Jamie was elated to see Ricky. Ricky greeted him as he crossed the street. Ricky said, "Hey man, we have some grown-up business to take care of today, so hop in. We are going to the bank to open up that bank account I promised for your birthday." Trying to sound real grown up, Jamie replied, "I am starting to be a man now right? Cause I gotta take care of Momma and I need money in the bank, right?"

"Yeah, Little Man," Ricky responded smiling as he playfully poked Jamie on the shoulder.

In the meantime, Ms. King was getting very worried because Jamie had not gotten home from the bus stop yet. It was now 3:20 PM and he usually arrived at 3:05 PM. Ms. King was very concerned and called Teresa.

"Oh, I am sorry Momma King. He is with Ricky. I should have told you myself. I had assumed Ricky would have stopped in to tell you that he was picking up Jamie. He is opening a savings account for Jamie for his birthday! Isn't that really sweet of Ricky? He loves Jamie as his very own. He is really a wonderful man," Teresa declared proudly with excitement. Teresa never knew that Ricky had vowed to himself that he would never set foot in Ms.

King's house again. It was something he could not explain even to himself but he felt extremely uncomfortable in her presence.

"Yes, that is very nice Teresa, but be careful," Momma King warned. "Something just does not seem right for some reason."

"Oh, Momma King! You worry too much. I know how much you love Jamie and are so protective of him," she teased. "All is well. Have a good evening, Momma King. We love you."

Ms. Joni King was like a grandmother to Jamie. She had cared for him since he was born and loved him as her own. Ms. King was a very attractive widow woman in her early sixties. She was always neatly dressed, with shiny silver hair that hung loosely down her back in a ponytail or sometimes pinned-up in a bun on the top of her head. She never remarried after her husband, Harold, died in a car accident many years prior.

She was elated that Teresa asked her to babysit for Jamie shortly after he was born. Teresa had to return to work and knew Momma King would be an excellent choice to care for Jamie. Although Ms. King did not have children of her own, many of the neighborhood kids were always stopping by or running small errands for her.

Ms. King was a very kind, God-fearing woman who spent most of her time in the evenings at church or praying and reading the Word of God. She often would tell Jamie Bible stories and read to him. Jamie loved spending time with Ms. King after school. She always had lots of goodies for him. He enjoyed the nicely scented oil she would put on his forehead and the way she would pray to God in another language. Jamie never really understood it, but it always made him feel warm and tingly inside. He always wanted his mother to go over to Ms. King to have some oil put on her to make her feel warm and tingly inside too. His mom always seemed sad until Ricky started coming around.

Once, when Teresa stopped by Momma King to pick up Jamie, she invited Ricky in to meet her. She had seen them together on numerous occasions and noticed that Teresa appeared very happy. Teresa was beaming from ear to ear as she introduced Ricky. As Momma King extended her hand, Ricky took her hand in his, but instantly dropped it. He suddenly did not feel very well and wanted to leave her presence immediately. In fact, he told Teresa he would wait for her outside, calling for Jamie to join him. Teresa stood very perplexed and embarrassed as she gazed into Momma King's face for some sort of explanation. Ricky had always been a perfect gentleman with a voluble personality. He was a great conversationalist and fun to be around. This was not the Ricky she had known. "What had just happened?" she questioned.

Teresa, feeling very awkward said, "I am so sorry Momma King, I don't even know what to say." Momma King smiled and gently lifted her chin. She looked deeply into her eyes and said, "My dear child, how well do you know him?"

Teresa, sounding defensive, replied, "I have known him since high school, and why do you ask?"

"My dear child, I can sense you love him deeply, but just remember that sometimes people are not always who they appear to be. I just want you to be careful and pay attention to everything about him." She leaned forward and kissed Teresa on her forehead.

CHAPTER 10

Sal parked his car in the designated parking space at the complex where he had once lived with Carolyn. Suddenly he did not know what he would say to her. His heart was beating fast, with each thump sounding loudly in his ears. He was paralyzed with fear. What if Carolyn rejects him? What if she had met someone else? What if she refuses to even talk to him? Taking a deep breath, he exhaled slowly to calm his nerves and to slow down his heartbeat. Several minutes passed and without hesitation, he opened the car door and quickly walked to the apartment complex.

As he approached Carolyn's apartment, his legs began to wobble and he felt nervous and weak. Even though he still had the keys, he knocked softly on the door. Carolyn looked through the peep hole, quickly opened the door, and yanked him into the apartment. So happy to see him, she began to cry tears of joy as she hugged and kissed him. They both cried and kissed and held each other for several minutes before ever speaking a word to each other.

In unison, they whispered. "I am sorry."

They spent the rest of the evening getting caught up and making passionate love as never before. They discussed everything from the day she came home and found him in bed with Margie. They discussed the altercation she had with Margie and the shocking news that nothing actually happened between the two of them. He shared with her the emptiness, the frustrations and vulnerability he felt not being able to provide for her as a man. Carolyn assured Sal that there would never be a need for another woman as long as she was alive and well. He teased her about the egg he had on the back of his head for several weeks, and how thankful he was that they never owned a gun.

After a hot shower together, they made sandwiches and each enjoyed a hot cup of tea. Sal shared with Carolyn about his job driving and delivering pillows for Paradise and how his job required him to make runs to designated hubs. He explained that sometimes he would not be able to make it back home depending on where he had to go. She did not care as long as he was coming home. Sal was so happy. He told Carolyn that he had been doing some things he had never really done before and he wanted her to be a part of it. Carolyn suddenly became suspicious and showed serious concern, not able to imagine what he had been doing. "Is it something illegal?" she inquired. She just could not imagine what he could be talking about.

Seeing the fear on her face, he quickly laughed and with a sheepish grin said, "I have been talking to God." Sal was not sure of her reaction and he quickly repeated it. "I have been praying and I believe God listens to me. He has done just what I have asked Him and I want us to talk to God together." Carolyn waved him off not sure how to respond. She had not given God much thought and she did not want to think about that now. She had Sal on her mind and a lot of making up to do. Sal did not push the issue and instead went with the flow as she took his hand and led him to the bedroom for the second time. They spent the weekend getting reacquainted and getting caught up on the months of separation.

CHAPTER 11

The sirens of the ambulance could be heard for blocks as they approached Lil Lady Elite restaurant. "Thank God they are here," as Lola sighed a sound of relief and whispered a little prayer. *"Dear God, please let Nate be okay,"* as she continued to brush back his damp sweaty hair. Reassuring him that he was going to be fine was equally comforting to her as well. A large crowd had gathered inside and outside of the restaurant. They watched with great concern and hoped all would be fine with Nate.

Nate and Lola Bishop were pillars in the community for years and were greatly respected. The two paramedics moved swiftly through the crowd with a gurney, asking people to please clear the aisles and the area as they reached Nate and began to assess the situation. They quickly asked Lola a few questions, took Nate's vitals and promptly placed him on the gurney to transport him to the hospital. Lola climbed in the back of the ambulance with Nate and one of the paramedics. They had called ahead to Morton's Hospital informing the staff that it was Nate Bishop. The nurses and doctors were waiting as they arrived.

After several hours of many tests and still not being able to diagnose the problem, the doctors decided that Nate should spend the night for observation. He was given a mild sedative to help make him sleep. Nate, now alert and feeling much better, tried to convince Lola that it may have been food poisoning from a turkey salad sandwich he had eaten earlier for lunch. He suggested she go home and get some rest. Lola, not buying his story, was definitely not leaving him. She knew there was something more, but wondered what could it be that could have devastated him in such a way? Lola, smiled and reassured Nate that he was probably right and would probably be able to go home the next day. She sat quietly by his bedside and held his hand. He was soon fast asleep.

However, Lola's mind would not shut-down. Her thoughts were everywhere, trying to reflect back on anything that Nate may have said or something strange or peculiar that happened she may have overlooked. She could not think of anything. She needed answers and was determined to find out what was going on with Nate. Her head was aching, so she took a Tylenol and an extra pillow to rest her head. She too, was soon fast asleep sitting in a chair, holding Nate's hand. She refused to go to the hospital suite where companions stayed overnight because she wanted to stay close to Nate; and, she did just that. She never left his side.

CHAPTER 12

Ricky felt relieved as Sal delivered the last of the shipment. It had finally arrived. The biggest and most profitable of the past two years. Nervous and excited, Ricky called each of the *BOYS* individually to confirm all was well and that he would be meeting with his contact on Sunday. Dante and Billy were well informed regarding the plan and of the key people involved. Each knew the plan as well as the other, even including a *Plan B* if it needed to be implemented. Ricky chose Sunday to make the exchange because no one would be at the warehouse at that time.

The past two days were very important for putting things in order. Ricky deposited five thousand dollars into the bank account he had opened in Jamie's name, with Billy's address and Billy's name as beneficiary, on Friday afternoon. Teresa was not aware that he had also opened a business account in her name with another five thousand dollars, using Dante's address in Florida and designating Dante as beneficiary. Ricky wanted all correspondence from the bank to go directly to the *BOYS* so no one would be the wiser. He did not put his name on anything. There would be nothing to connect him, but he would benefit all the same because they always looked out for each other.

Teresa was naive and gullible, she was very easily convinced by anything Ricky told her. She trusted him totally. Ricky boasted to the *BOYS* how it was so easy to get Teresa's social security number from the office files since he was well trusted and certainly no one would ever question him, not even Nate. He boasted how he told Teresa to make special labels marked *BOYS* so he could differentiate his labels from those of the company. Ricky told her that he wanted to ship packages to his *BOYS* and sometimes they needed to ship things to him, and he preferred not to get Nate involved. She quickly agreed and said, "No problem and no need to get Nate involved. He would not mind," as she smiled. "Anything for you baby."

He spent that Saturday going over the plan in his mind while he was fishing with Jamie. He loved the quietness and the fresh air outside the city limits. He could think more clearly. After he took Jamie home, he decided to go to check on the shipment at the warehouse, telling Teresa he would be back in an hour to take them out for dinner.

As he unlocked the warehouse, Ricky noticed that some boxes in the fourth sections where the *BOYS* shipment was seemed to have been moved from where he strategically left them. He moved closer to examine the boxes and discovered one box had fallen over and several pillow cases containing cocaine were visible. Ricky assumed that when Sal was stacking them in the warehouse, he did not balance each box on top of the other well enough and they fell over. Ricky was so happy that he had returned to check on things before it could be discovered by someone, because no one ever went to the warehouse after hours.

Nate trusted Ricky and relied on him as his right hand man. Ricky always gave him a full report on everything. Ricky knew Nate would not come to the warehouse. He knew that Sal did not have a key to the warehouse, so he too would not come. And even though Teresa had a key, she would not go on a Saturday. Ricky laughed and called himself a *paranoid gangster* as he stacked the boxes again. Besides, he figured to himself, only one more day and all will be changed forever, for him and the *BOYS*. Pick-up was scheduled for Sunday, since no one would be around and no one would know anything about the shipment. Monday morning it would be business as usual. Ricky smiled at his own brilliance.

****

Dr. Drew was a tall thin man in his late forties, with a robust voice and warm captivating blue eyes. He was known for his excellent bed-side manner and genuine concern for his patients. He had been Nate and Lola's doctor since he began his practice about twelve years earlier. He tapped softly on the door before quietly entering. Nate and Lola searched his eyes for any tell-tale signs regarding Nate's condition.

Sensing their deep concern, he immediately smiled and stated, "Every test we ran came back negative, so I want you to take it easy for the next few days and if you feel any discomfort, no matter how small it may be, do not hesitate, please call me right away. For now, it looks like you had an anxiety attack, but that is usually brought on by stress, or some shocking news of some sort." Nate laughed nervously, (reflecting on the emotional shock of his discovery) and tried to reassure Lola that he was fine and that there was nothing for her to worry about. Dr. Drew moved methodically and swiftly as he checked Nate's vitals and decided he could go home. He again reiterated that if there was any discomfort, dizziness, or numbness to call him immediately. Lola was taking it all in when she realized they did not have a car. It had been left at the Lil Lady Elite Restaurant. Since it was Saturday, everyone was out either running errands or cleaning. She was not sure who she could call to pick them up. After a brief debate within herself, she excused herself and went to the nurse's station and called a taxi.

Nate and Lola arrived at Lil Lady Elite late in the afternoon and decided to have a light lunch before returning home. Lola was determined to get some answers over lunch as to what could have upset Nate so much as to cause an anxiety attack. Nate appears to be himself, she thought, but wondered if it was all a disguise to keep her in the dark.

Nate spent the rest of the weekend assuring Lola that he was fine and all was well. Lola watched him carefully and agreed with him late Sunday night that he could go to work Monday morning. He promised that if he felt anything in the way of not feeling well, he would call her immediately and report to the hospital where she would meet him. Lola felt a little better about Nate's condition but was still convinced he was withholding something or some things. Perhaps he would discuss it with her later. She only hoped and believed whatever it was, would soon be resolved.

CHAPTER 13

Although Teresa loved and respected Momma King and often thought of her as a second mother, she felt Momma King had no basis for her warnings concerning Ricky. "She did not even know him and only met him once, so how could she really say such things." She repeated to herself. Teresa was convinced that she knew Ricky and loved him and that he loved her and Jamie. She believed Ricky would never do anything to hurt them. They were a family.

Ms. King was troubled in her spirit. She knew something was wrong, but didn't know what. After returning home from Bible Study that evening, she made a hot cup of tea and sat down at her kitchen table. As she began to quiet her spirit, she became instantly aware of this still small voice speaking within her saying, *"Call unto Me, and I will answer thee and show you great and mighty things that you know not."*

Ms. King immediately remembered that passage of scripture was written in the book of Jeremiah, Chapter 33 and verse 3. Without hesitation, she began to worship God, and praise Him. She began to call on the Name of Jesus, the Name above all Names. As she lay prostrate on the floor, she entered into a place of rest and peace as she continued to call on Jesus asking, "What is it Lord?" It was then that she saw Jamie and Teresa in the spirit realm, being pulled by an unseen force. It was pulling them into an old, very dark, dingy, dilapidated house. Ms. King could sense they were being led into a place of danger and darkness. Crying out and praying fervently, she began to bind the forces of darkness that were pulling them. Suddenly, her eyes were open and she was seeing in the supernatural, the evil forces that were attacking Jamie and Teresa. She began to pray more intensely, binding the forces of darkness and pleading the Blood of Jesus over them. She could see into the spirit realm that the more intense her prayers, the more the forces of darkness began backing up, hissing and cursing. The evil forces were reaching for them but not able to touch them. Ms. King did not stop praying for several hours until she began to feel peaceful again. She knew that whatever Jamie and Teresa were encountering or were about to encounter, that fervent effectual prayer would change it.

Ms. King got up from the kitchen floor, reheated her cup of tea, and continued to give God thanks for His gifts that He had bestowed upon her. She was so humbled and thankful to God for filling her with His Spirit and showing her things about which she knew nothing. She felt so warm and secure to know that God was always with her and loved her so much. She began to weep softly as she felt a warmth that seemed to be like hot oil flowing from the top of her head down over her body that spoke, *"Yes, my darling daughter, I love you with an everlasting love. I will never leave you or forsake you."*

Ms. King learned how to pray when her beloved Harold was killed in a tragic car accident a few years prior. She did not think she could make it without him. His loss was almost too hard for her to bear. The pain in her heart had made her feel empty, depressed and sad. She was always asking God, "Why, why God did you take the love of my life?" She wanted answers. She believed in God, but did not have a close relationship with Him at the time. She decided to go to church to find out how a "supposedly loving" God could take her Harold. It just did not make any sense to her. She was alone and hurting badly. She began to go faithfully every time the church doors were open. Bible Study and Sunday School were her favorite. She asked everyone she knew, including the pastor, "Why would God take my Harold and leave me all alone?"

There was never an answer that satisfied her. Many of the parishioners grew to love Mother King. Some genuinely felt her pain and empathized with her.

Ms. King then decided, "Why ask them? Why not ask God Himself?" This was always taught in church; that God wants to have a personal relationship with each of us and He speaks to us. She never really talked to God until Harold died and never thought it was possible to have the Almighty God stop what He was doing to speak to her. How insignificant she once felt.

One evening after Bible Study, Ms. King could not turn Pastor Sherman's voice off in her head. Ms. King was hearing over and over again, Pastor saying, *"God created you to have fellowship with Him. You were created to worship God and bring Him glory and honor. God formed you in your mother's womb for His purpose. He has a plan for you. His thoughts towards you are good, even though bad things can happen. It is part of the purpose. When you trust God, there is no pain without a purpose. There is a reason for all things. Your existence is not a mistake. Seek His face and find your purpose in life."* Ms. King began to think out loud asking God, "Did Harold fulfill his purpose? What is my purpose? How do I seek you God? How do I have fellowship with you?" Ms. King was full of questions and was not ashamed to ask. Every thought that came to her mind, she would ask God. Looking at her Bible she quickly opened it and immediately her eyes fell on the passage of Scripture in *James 4:8, "If you draw close to me, I will draw close to you."* That spoke such volumes to her heart that it changed her life forever. She knew God spoke to her. She believed all of the answers to her questions were in that book. She drew closer and began to study the Word of God. She would spend many hours talking to God and many times after speaking with Him, she would find the answers to her questions in the Bible. She desired more, because each time she prayed and read the Word of God, she always had a longing for more. Ms. King began to understand that she was having fellowship with God. She was comforted and changed. She worshipped Him and honored Him by trying to live the lifestyle that Jesus exemplified in the Bible. She realized that worshipping God was a way of life. It was not just an *"on Sunday"* experience, but every day, the body, mind and soul must be presented to God as a living sacrifice to please Him.

A few months later, Ms. King read in *Matthew 7:11, "If you being evil know how to give good gifts to your children, how much more will your Heavenly Father give the Holy Spirit to those who ask?"* Ms. King wanted more and asked God to fill her with His Holy Spirit. She did not know what to expect, but as she began to praise God, she was suddenly speaking in a language she did not know and once again she experienced something that felt like warm oil being poured over her. The language was so melodious to her ears that she actually thought she was dreaming. She spoke in her new language for several minutes. As she picked up her Bible, she turned to the Book of Acts, the second chapter, and read where the disciples were filled with the Holy Spirit and spoke in unknown tongues. She knew God had deliberately directed her to those passages. Ms. King had joy unspeakable and felt absolutely amazing! She loved this experience more than anything she had ever experienced before in her life. She knew she was changed from the inside out.

One evening as she was lying in bed, she asked God, "Why did you take Harold from me? Did he fulfill the purpose You had for his life?"

As she sat still listening for that small voice, she heard so clearly, *"Yes, my daughter, Harold is with Me now and he fulfilled his purpose. If I had not allowed this tragedy, you would have never come to know Me. See, through this pain and tragedy, you sought Me and now you have found Me. I was with you in your time of pain and sorrow. I had to let you feel this pain. If not, you would have never surrendered your life to Me and would have been lost for eternity. You are Mine now and I will never let you go. My daughter, you are so precious to Me and I love you with an everlasting love and nothing can ever change that."*

Ms. King felt so special as she drifted off to sleep, it was as if Jesus himself were holding her in His arms, rocking her into a peaceful bliss like none other.

CHAPTER 14

Ricky was being his charming self at dinner with Teresa and Jamie, when his beeper went off. Ricky immediately excused himself and went outside to call whomever it was that beeped him. Teresa tried to act as if it were okay, but even Jamie was curious as to whom Ricky could be talking to in private. Something suddenly did not feel right to Teresa. Was there another woman? What was Ricky hiding from her?

"Hey Man, its Dante. Big Mc can't make the Pick-up on Sunday as planned. He had to have his gall bladder removed and there was some complications. Will it be okay to leave *it* there for a few more days?" he asked. "Big Mc should be able to do business as we all planned in a few days. You know Big Mc does not trust anyone to make *this* Pick-up but himself. Are you okay with that Man?"

Ricky did not answer Dante, but instead he asked, "Did you discuss this with Billy?"

"Yeah Man, he is cool with it, if you are okay with it" Dante stated.

"Yeah Man, it's cool. It's safe, but the sooner the better," said Ricky.

Ricky stood stunned by the news and hoped no one would discover the contents of the warehouse. He thought about Big Mc and hoped things would be okay for his sake as well as the whole plan.

McKenzie Moore AKA Big Mc was a powerful charismatic man, but an infamous criminal, who was feared and respected by many on the streets of New York City. He was the connection and main contact for nearly all the big drug trafficking from New York to Florida. He often frequented The Oasis Nightclub and had his own VIP section just for him and his private guests. He always had to keep a low profile. Dante, Ricky and Billy had been out clubbing, and celebrating each other as they always had, buying drinks for all, and leaving large tips when they first met Big Mc. They had a reputation as well-to-do men, but no one could ever say what they did for a living. They just always seemed to have lots of women, money and were always well dressed. Big Mc would sit back and observe them most of the night as he had done for several months through the double one way glass. One night, as they were about to leave, Big Mc buzzed Rachel, the bartender, to tell

Ricky he wanted to talk with him and his friends. Ricky had heard of Big Mc but had never met him. He felt proud to meet the most feared and yet respected man alive in New York City.

They joined Big Mc with a few of his boys in the VIP room in the back, behind the bar. "I have been watching you guys many nights from here and I like your swag. You guys are smooth and got style. I am Big Mc and this is JayZ, MoJo, Howie, and Dwayne." Each man acknowledged each other with a head nod. "We are building an empire here in New York and along the east coast to Florida and are looking for men with swag who want to make some big money...Interested?"

Ricky spoke up, "Exactly what are you doing to build an empire in New York and along the east coast to Florida?"

Big Mc said, "Let's meet back here next Saturday night and we can discuss more details. Right now I want to know if you guys are at least interested." Ricky made eye contact with Dante and Billy. They knew each other very well and understood their unspoken body language. They were interested, and each agreed and shook hands.

Big Mc had his designated law enforcers check on their background to see if they were just what he had observed them to be, small time hustlers with small rap sheets. Big Mc had connections with many influential people, some law enforcers, politicians, business owners who occasionally did favors for him, and for whom he did favors in return.

That was almost three years ago, and Billy and Dante had since relocated.

CHAPTER 15

Ricky's demeanor was jovial and upbeat as he apologized to Teresa and Jamie for leaving the table to make the call. He told them that his friend in Texas was having some personal problems and he was trying to help him but did not want to upset or involve them. Teresa gobbled up his lies along with her dinner and believed him wholeheartedly. After all, why would she believe differently? She never even considered the warning from Momma King.

They had their usual small talk conversations and flirted with each other while Jamie seemed to be occupied with his food. Ricky wanted to call it an early night because he had some thinking to do, but did not want to create any suspicion with Teresa. After dinner, Teresa did notice that he seemed to drift away a few times and was not giving her his undivided attention as he always did. Ricky said he was a little tired and wanted to get back to his apartment, but promised to tuck Jamie in. Teresa rationalized within herself that his inattentiveness was because he was tired and worried about his friend. She wondered if she might be able to talk him into spending the night with her. She loved when he spent the night. Those times seemed like they were a real family. She never wanted to be too forward or aggressive, but she often dreamed about when Ricky would marry her. He never brought up the subject and when she would casually mention a deeper commitment, he would change the subject or say, "I love what we have now. Sometimes marriage puts a strain on a relationship and right now I don't want to take that chance."

Things had been running pretty smoothly, including Ricky's employment with Paradise Pillows. Ricky thought his access to the warehouse would be the perfect cover for Big Mc and the *BOYS* to smuggle anything and everything. On several occasions Ricky and the *BOYS* smuggled weapons, furs, diamonds, and jewelry for Big Mc through Paradise Pillows. A perfect set up, and all was working out very well until Police Chief Dan Waters retired and was replaced by a newcomer to town named, Police Chief Barry 'Hawkeye' Lee, from Miami, Florida.

CHAPTER 16

Police Chief Waters was elated to retire, and felt so relieved that he no longer had to look the other way because of the negative influence and manipulation Big Mc had on him. Chief Waters was being blackmailed by Big Mc because of his infidelity. Big Mc knew Chief Waters was a married man with three adult children who also held very reputable positions in the community as well. Unfortunately, Chief Waters had not considered his wife or his children's possible humiliation if he were caught. He only considered his great appetite for sexual favors from certain *high class call girls* who, unbeknownst to him, worked for Big Mc. Big Mc had quickly set up cameras and recorded several different sessions that Chief Waters had with three of his *favorite girls.* Big Mc copied the video and took it personally to Police Chief Waters at his office. Big Mc had told him to watch it in private and that he would be in touch with him in a few days.

Chief Waters had nervously locked his door to his office and put on the video. He tried hard to steady his breathing knowing intuitively that whatever was on the video was not going to be good. He never imagined it would be a video of his secret life with prostitutes. Chief Lee was mortified.

Big Mc then called two days later and spoke to Chief Waters saying, "All you have to do is look the other way and your secrets will never be revealed. Is that understood?"

Feeling totally subjugated and defeated, Waters managed to whisper, "Yes...Uh, understood."

Big Mc quickly hung up feeling satisfied for the opportunity to enlarge his territory of illegal dealings without incident.

Chief Waters wrestled with his conscience but then decided as long as he looked away, everything would be okay. He could still have his *favorite girls.* He smiled and thought, "This is a win-win situation for all involved. Big Mc gets what he wants and I get the *girls* and the *girls* get me."

That was five years ago and now that he was retiring, his running around days were over. He was content with that. Things were getting more and more complicated because he was not the *superman* he once thought he was five years earlier anyway. Because that part of his life was soon to be over and would be forgotten. He planned to spend more time at home with his wife, Peggy.

Chief Waters felt relieved that he never got caught. He was sometimes so ashamed of himself to have conducted himself as he did, and to have been manipulated and blackmailed by Big Mc. As the guilt and shame increased, his conscience began to bother him so much that he could not sleep. Many nights he tossed and turned as he heard himself taking his solemn pledge and vowed to protect and uphold the law, even if it meant his life. He had failed miserably as Police Chief for the last five years.

Now retired, this nagging in his mind was more poignant than when he was engaging in all sorts of immorality which was not appropriate for a man in his position. He thought to himself, "How can I get these dreams and images out of my mind? How could I have done such despicable things? What happened to my integrity? *"Oh God, help me! Forgive me please!"* Overwhelmed by his guilt and emotions, Chief Waters heard a voice that seemed to permeate from within himself say, *"Your conscience is greater than your sins. Repent, for the Kingdom of God is at hand."* There was no doubt, Chief Waters knew it was God speaking to him. He humbled himself and cried like a baby asking God to forgive him for his betrayal and for being a low-down dirty disgrace of a man. The more he cried, the lighter he felt. Finally, his burden of guilt was no more. He had an encounter which shook him to the very core of his being. When the tears finally subsided about two hours later, he knew he was a changed man. He could not articulate what had happened, but something wonderful took place. He felt changed, regenerated, born-again and renewed.

He now decided that there were things he must get right and it would start on Monday. He determined, "I will stop by the office to see the new Police Chief, Barry Lee."

CHAPTER 17

Nate Bishop and Sal arrived at Paradise Pillow at the same time Monday morning. Nate thought that it was a great time to ask Sal about the shipment he saw in the warehouse. Sal had only met Nate once which was when he was first hired. He knew Nate was the owner, but felt a greater loyalty to Ricky, since Ricky had given him the job.

Sal approached Nate as he stepped out of his car. Nate cautiously smiled and said, "Good morning Sal, nice sun shiny day huh?"

"Oh yes Mr. Bishop, very lovely day indeed," as they both began to walk toward the office.

"So you are the new driver that delivers to various hubs, right?" Nate asked nonchalantly.

"Oh yes. Ricky gives me designated places to drop-off and pick-up."

"You pick up deliveries too?" queried Nate. Sal nodded his head.

"Oh, and the deliveries you pick up, you bring back here to the warehouse?" Nate continued.

"Yes, I just picked up a delivery on Friday and Ricky told me where to stack it in the warehouse as always because he likes to keep it organized."

Nate smiled and said, "Yes, Ricky is a great organizer, but one more question. Where did you get the last shipment you delivered here on Friday?"

"Oh, that shipment came in from Miami, Florida. Is everything okay, Mr. Bishop?" Sal asked, starting to feel a little uncomfortable with the many questions.

"Oh yes. I wanted you to know that I appreciate the job you have been doing. So, you and Ricky went to school together huh?" Nate was deliberately fishing for information to determine if Sal was knowingly involved in the shipment of drugs in his warehouse.

"Oh, no, I met Ricky a couple of months ago. I was homeless and sleeping in my car in the back near your warehouse. He offered me a job as a driver. I was so grateful. He is such a great guy. His offering me this job saved my marriage and renewed my relationship with God. Do you believe in God, Mr. Bishop?"

Nate smiled nodding his head and said, "All my life I believed in God but never really prayed to Him until just a few days ago." Nate thought of that day in the hospital when he was under observation from his panic attack. He was in deep thought as Sal opened the door to the office and headed to the Maintenance Room to wait for Ricky.

"It was nice speaking with you Mr. Bishop. Have a great day," Sal said.

Nate waved and nodded again as he unlocked his office door and turned on his coffee maker. Teresa was always so efficient in setting things up the night before so all that was needed was to turn the switch.

There was so much running through Nate's mind; he had to figure out how and whom to approach. Should he call the police and get them involved? How would he explain it to them? Would they believe him? In his brief conversation with Sal, he knew Sal was not the culprit and had no knowledge of what was going on.

Nate sat at his desk in deep thought when Teresa came through the office door, and as usual, she poked her head into his office, and yelled, "Good morning Nate! How was your weekend?"

Nate did not answer his usual, "All was well. Great weekend with a great wife...and you?" but instead, he uttered, "When you put your things down, would you come see me?"

Teresa was puzzled and somewhat perplexed. Nate had a look on his face she had never seen before, kind of scary, serious and confused all at once. "Uh, yes. Sure, I will be right there," Teresa said.

Teresa quickly dropped her things at her work station and grabbed her notepad just in case she needed to take some notes. She knocked lightly on the door and walked in.

"Good morning Nate. Is everything okay?" she inquired, with great concern.

Nate said, "Well I had a very interesting weekend. I was hospitalized but I am feeling better today."

"Really Nate, what happened? Are you okay?" Teresa's eyes softened and were suddenly full of love and compassion for her boss whom she had grown to cherish as family. Nate was carefully watching for any sign of deception, but there were none. He decided not to tell of his *findings* in the warehouse, but he did want to get a few answers.

"Yes, Teresa I am fine. I felt light-headed last Friday evening when I took Lola out to dinner and then passed out. I spent the night in the hospital for observation and was discharged the next day with a clean bill of health. I am fine, but I need to take it easy for a few days. And oh, by the way, before leaving last Friday, I was checking the last shipment that was delivered and I noticed how well the warehouse was organized. Did Ricky organize it himself?" he inquired, trying to look pleased.

"Yes, Nate, I believe so. He told me he wanted to reorganize and asked me to make labels on some of the boxes marked *BOYS.*"

"Oh, yes," Nate asked, "Why did you make those labels? What does *BOYS* mean?"

Teresa remembered agreeing with Ricky not to say anything to Nate. She thought it was no big deal to have Ricky's family and friends send things back and forth, since they already had to deliver pillows to Chicago, Texas, Florida, and New York anyway. But was it okay not to say anything to Nate? Teresa questioned herself.

Teresa had always been a loyal employee and Nate trusted her totally. Teresa, suddenly feeling a bit uncomfortable but not really sure why, smiled at Nate.

"Well, shortly after Ricky started working here, he asked me to make some extra labels because he had family he wanted to keep in touch with and send things to when we made deliveries. Sometimes he would send things to them and they would send things back. To distinguish his boxes from ours, he would label his *BOYS*. I did not see any harm in it since we had to transport the deliveries anyway." Nate did not appear to be too pleased with her answer.

Teresa quickly added, "Did I do something wrong, Nate?"

"No, you did nothing wrong, but I am disappointed that you did not inform me, that's all. Do you have any idea as to what was being shipped from here, or being received here?"

"No and I never thought about it further," she said. "I am so sorry Nate. I would never do anything deliberately to disappoint you. You are right. I should have cleared this with you first."

Nate took Teresa's hand in his and looked into her eyes to assure her that it was okay and not to worry.

"But I need to ask you to not share this with anyone," Nate implored.

Teresa, perplexed and confused asked, "What should I not share with anyone? My making extra labels, or Ricky sending packages to his friends and family?" she asked.

Nate, for the first time, saw Teresa's vulnerability and naiveté. He realized he needed to be explicit and direct.

"Please, do not mention our conversation with anyone, not even your boyfriend Ricky until further notice. Will you promise me that Teresa?"

"Yes Nate, of course," as she gazed shyly into his eyes, "I promise." While Teresa turned to walk out of his office she heard the front office door close.

Strong and solid footsteps approached Nate's office, just as she was exiting.

"Oh, good morning Ricky," Teresa uttered, trying to smile and look cheerful as always.

"Buongiorno Bella Teresa," in his poor version of Italian, that meant, "Good morning, Beautiful." He was a real Casanova and quite a charmer. Teresa blushed and laughed softly as she walked down the hall to her work station.

Ricky poked his head into Nate's office and said, "Good morning Nate. Nice to see you." Nate mustered a smile and waved him off as if he were in deep thought and pre-occupied, pretending he was looking in the folder he had on his desk.

As Ricky turned to follow Teresa down the hall, Nate yelled, "Oh Ricky, could you come back to my office around two this afternoon?"

"Sure," Ricky said. "No problem. See you then."

Everything seemed pretty normal to Ricky as he winked at Teresa when he passed her work station on his way to his office in the maintenance department.

CHAPTER 18

"Oh good morning, Sal. You are here early today," Ricky said smiling.

"Yeah Boss, I wanted to ask if you would be needing me the next few days to make a delivery?" He stood and shook Ricky's hand.

Ricky smiled, "No, actually the delivery you made Friday was good for a few days. Why? Do you need some time off?"

"Yeah," Sal smiled, "I want to surprise my lady and take her to the Poconos for a few days. I never realized how much I really loved her until the day she caught me in a compromising situation with another woman and ran me out of the house."

Ricky started smirking, "Man, you mean you got caught? I gotta teach you a few things. Man, you can't be a player with real swag and get caught!"

Sal said, "Yeah Man, I had never really cheated on my wife, and if she had not come home when she had, it would have gone down." Sal spoke in a monotone voice as he vividly recalled the incident and shared it with Ricky.

Ricky laughed, "Man, no, not in your own house in your own bed and she clobbered you with a rolling pin? No! No! No! No!" he exclaimed as he fell backward in his oversized plush leather chair laughing hysterically. "I can't believe you would be that stupid. Man, I really gotta teach you a few things. Yeah Man, you go on and take care of your business and when you come back, I am gonna give you a few pointers."

Sal snapped out of the horrible nightmare as he remembered it. He walked over to Ricky's desk looked him squarely in the eyes and said, "No, Man, that will not be necessary. I will never cheat on my wife, because I truly love her and she is deserving of a man that will honor her and respect her. So, no thanks, but I would like to share with you some things I recently experienced. I never told you what happened before you offered me this job to drive for Paradise Pillows, did I?"

Before Ricky could answer, Sal interjected. "Ricky, you may not know this, but God used you to change my life in so many ways! I first prayed, and asked God to help me as I fell asleep for the second night in my car, repenting for what I had done. I asked God for another chance to make things right with my wife. I was homeless, Man, with no money, no shoes, no job, and then the next day you gave me a job, shoes, and a week's salary in advance. I realized that God heard my prayers and now just recently gave me a second chance with my wife. I promised her and God that I would honor and respect her as I should and that is what I plan to do for the rest of my life. Man, that's what you do when you love someone and respect them. I love her and I love God. God fixed both my marriage and me as a man."

Ricky did not know what to say or do, but he felt real compassion for the first time. Sal's eyes filled with tears as he continued. "I have struggled all my life, feeling rejected because of the abuse I suffered as a young boy. I considered and labeled myself a loser. My father was an alcoholic and always wanted to use me as his punching bag. My mother was beaten severely for trying to shield me from him in his drunken rampages," he paused, choking on his tears. "She died of a heart attack trying to protect me from him. I spent my entire childhood trying to protect my mother from my father and I failed. When I turned 13 years old, I ran away from home and my father's abuse. I was filled with so much rage and anger and got into a lot of street fights. I had trust issues and thought everyone wanted to hurt me. It was by the Grace of God that I was never incarcerated or arrested. It was extremely hard trying to find shelter every day. Sometimes I slept in parks and vacant buildings. I would spend most of the day trying to find food. I tried to run far away from the image of my mother's bruised body, blackened eyes, and swollen face. Her face would follow me everywhere all the time. I felt responsible for her death. I was ashamed of myself until I met my wife, Carolyn, ten years ago. She understood me and encouraged me. That's why I felt such guilt for being in that compromising situation. She made me the man I am today. And now as a man, I will spend the rest of my life protecting and loving her as she deserves."

With tears running down his face, Sal suddenly was aware that Ricky was speechless and crying too! They hugged each other and Ricky said, "Man, I am sorry. I'm sorry Man. Really, I did not know... I'm so sorry."

"No problem, but I never got to tell you the difference you made in my life and I appreciate you Man. Thanks so much," said Sal.

Ricky, feeling weak and soft, said, "You're welcome, Man. You're welcome. We can talk more when you come back. Enjoy your time with your wife in the Poconos, Man," as Ricky guided Sal towards the door. Sal had no choice but to follow. They shook hands again.

Ricky walked back to his desk and flopped in his chair with a thud. What just happened? He had never felt so emotional. It was as though he realized he had a heart that could really care. He had never felt so much compassion before. What would the *BOYS* think of this scene? Slick Ricky, soft and crying? Really?

****

Nate sat pondering about what to do next, and then decided he would call his old friend, former Chief Police Dan Waters. Nate and Lola had attended his retirement party and promised to keep in touch. "Now is a good time to make that call," Nate thought. Nate wanted both his advice as well as someone to confide in. He found Chief Waters' number in his huge black book with hundreds of contacts and decided he would give him a call before he would confront Ricky at two o'clock.

"Hello Dan, this is Nate Bishop. How are you doing?"

"Oh, I'm doing well. I just left the station. I was talking to the new Chief, Barry Lee about a few unresolved matters," Dan said feeling a tinge of guilt. "It is hard to believe I am officially retired."

"Yes, I understand. After all, you have been in law enforcement over thirty years. That is a long time," Nate affirmed.

"Yeah, kinda hard getting into a *retired routine.*"

They both laughed.

Nate said, "Well I was wondering if you could meet me at Lil Lady Elite for lunch around 11:30? I would like your advice on a matter."

"Oh sure, I have nothing but lots of time now," he chuckled, "Well, it is about 9:30 now, so I'll see you there in a couple of hours."

"Thanks so much Dan, I really appreciate it. See you then," said Nate.

"Yeah, sure thing goodbye," said Dan.

Nate hung up the phone questioning himself if this was the right thing to do. Speaking out loud to himself. "Well, we will know soon enough."

****

Dante had just gotten word from Big Mc that he would pick up the shipment on Tuesday and to get the word to Ricky. Big Mc would only contact Dante to keep his involvement at a minimal with Ricky, just in case the authorities tried to connect the dots. Ricky was startled by the phone ringing as he was still thinking of the effect Sal's conversation had on him.

"Hello, Maintenance, Ricky speaking."

"Hey Man, it's me," Dante said, without identifying himself.

"Is Tuesday at 6 AM good for the Pick-up?"

"Yeah Man, Tuesday at 6 AM is cool. No one is around at that time. Yeah Man, all is well and going as planned. Deposit should be made by noon on Tuesday, after the Pick-up," Ricky said smiling. "Payday tomorrow!"

CHAPTER 19

Police Chief Barry Lee was an interesting person. He was in his early forties, never married and had no children. He was very nerdy, with a muscular build that was easy to detect in any of his clothing. He was extremely devoted to his job and spent a lot of his free time in the gym. He loved to work off his stress by running on the treadmill and playing handball.

He moved up the ranks pretty quickly to police chief. He graduated from college with a degree in Criminal Justice at the top of his class and immediately started his own business as a private investigator. He had earned the nickname of 'Hawkeye' Lee in Miami as a private investigator for eight years. He was social when there was a need to be, but usually preferred to stay to himself with very few people in his inner circle of friends. Yet, because of his position, he was well liked and very much respected in the community. He had a way of making people feel very comfortable in his presence and easily made conversation with any stranger. He was exceptionally good at extracting information from anyone. People would automatically let down their guard and speak very freely with him. He made one feel like he was their very best friend and they could share anything and everything without being judged. He had a keen eye for details and scored exceptionally high among his peers in solving mysteries.

Oh yes, Chief Lee was good at his job. In fact, so good that the US Presidential Committee had sought him out to become a part of the Federal Law Judicial Security and Special Mission Enforcement Team. Barry Lee AKA 'Hawkeye' went undercover, gave up his private investigation practice and went through the intense training in Quantico, Virginia. He graduated at the top of his class. He was a natural leader and was assigned to work closely with the Police Commissioner in Miami, Major Collins and Chief of Police, Justin Skye, after graduation. Their staff was working diligently trying to track down the 'king pin' responsible for drug trafficking in Miami and now all their hard work was about to pay off.

Chief Lee joined the Commissioner and Police Chief Skye, when they called a meeting to brief the officers that an informant advised them of a big drug shipment that came into Florida three days prior and was taken to a warehouse in New York.

"I want each of you to keep your eyes and ears open. No lead is too small to follow. We have to find out who and where this shipment came from and who the person is on the receiving end. We have a description of a white van with a New York license plate and the name *Paradise* on the driver's door. We can do this guys, okay? Let's get to work," Chief Skye encouraged.

Chief Police Skye decided to contact the New York Police Department (NYPD) to give them the information and to make them aware of their findings.

"Hello, Chief Dan Waters speaking."

"Hello, Chief Waters. It is Chief Skye in Miami, Florida. How are things going?" he said.

"Well, things are well here. I am looking forward to retiring in a few months," Dan said smiling.

"Oh, really Man? That is great! Congratulations to you," said Justin. "Do you have a replacement yet?"

"No, I don't think so, but it will be a few months yet. I think the Police Commissioner may have someone in mind," Dan replied.

"Oh, that is good. Listen, I am calling to inform you that our investigation has led us to your neighborhood. We have a lead that someone in a big drug trafficking ring made a pick up here three days ago. We are looking for a white van with New York tags, and the name *Paradise* on the driver's door. We believe it was carrying a large quantity of drugs and it may be someplace in your neighborhood," Justin stated matter-of-factly. "Okay," Dan said, "I will brief my officers first thing tomorrow morning to be on the lookout. Thanks so much for calling."

"Yeah Chief, and if I don't speak with you again, congratulations on your retirement" said Justin, "And of course, if you see or hear anything, give me a call."

"Yes, yes of course," assured Dan, "Goodbye now."

They both hung up and sat at their desks, pondering what the other had said.

Chief Skye thought, "I wonder if Commissioner Collins knows Chief Waters is retiring. I will inform him tomorrow for sure. Perhaps if this case is not solved we could send 'Hawkeye' Lee. He could become the next Chief of Police when a few strings are pulled. We need someone in New York that we can trust and someone we know. There were rumors that Chief Waters maybe compromising his authority.

After hearing what Chief Skye shared, Chief Waters had a strong suspicion that it could be some of Big Mc thugs. "Well, whatever or whomever," he thought, "I will turn the other way and there will be no briefing in the morning to look out for a white van. Besides, I will be retiring in a few months and I just want to get out and away from everything, especially the crippling evidence Big Mc holds on me."

CHAPTER 20

It was three weeks before Police Chief Dan Waters actually retired, when Barry 'Hawkeye' Lee from Miami, Florida was introduced as the new police chief. Dan was extremely stressed those last three weeks. It was unnerving to have the new police chief so close to his illegal activities. He was more cautious about leaving his desk and drawers and files unlocked when not in use. Hawkeye Lee asked thousands of questions about his new job and his new staff, or so it seemed, and his eyes and ears were always open. Lee clearly noticed he was not privy to certain files and certain information.

"Chief Waters is obviously hiding something, but what? Now, I gotta find a way to get him to relax and make him feel like I am his friend, his best friend, so his guard comes down and I can extract some information," Lee thought to himself. "Maybe I will invite him out for dinner and a few drinks next week."

At the end of the second week, before Chief Waters retired, he was anxious to get with the *girls* for the last time. He felt sad, and yet very happy, because he no longer had to live this double lifestyle of lies and deception anymore. He wanted it to be very special for his *girls* and not the normal Friday night shenanigans. Thinking of something different and meaningful to do for this last time, he left his office and forgot to lock his desk.

Hawkeye Lee had just returned to the precinct late that afternoon to ask Chief Waters about getting together to have dinner one evening before retiring. Surprisingly, the door was unlocked, so he decided to go in and wait for him. He walked over to the window and noticed Chief Waters' car was not in his designated parking space. Assuming Chief Waters had gone home for the day, 'Hawkeye' quickly took advantage of this opportunity. He searched Chief Waters desk and read several incident reports. He pulled open the bottom drawer and wedged deep in the back, he discovered a video tape marked 'CONFIDENTIAL BY MM.' Hawkeye Lee quickly tucked it into the inside pocket of his London Fog topcoat, and continued looking. Satisfied and curious about his find, he retreated and left the office, eager to unfold the contents of the video.

Since it was Friday, Hawkeye Lee decided he would watch the contents of the video later that evening, after he returned from the gym. If it was something that needed divulging, the weekend would give him time to mull over his findings. His workouts were always therapeutic and he always insisted he was able to think better after a good workout. It was about 9 PM when Hawkeye settled down to watch the video. As he once again studied the video itself marked 'CONFIDENTIAL BY MM' in black marker. He thought about who "MM" could possibly be.

The video began with Chief Waters entering a hotel room. He quickly took a shower, and returned back in his boxer shorts. He appeared to be waiting for someone. He opened a chilled bottle of champagne that was obviously left for him and poured himself a drink. Chief lit the candles and put on some soft music and relaxed on the bed, as he sipped the champagne. Soon there was a knock on the door. Chief leaped from the bed to answer it.

Chief 'Hawkeye' Lee eyes bulged. He was shocked and very intrigued to see what would happen next. A tall slender lady with vivid red hair wearing a full length black coat tied at the waist greeted Chief with open arms. Chief pulled her close to him and kissed her while untying her coat, revealing her skimpy blouse, her tiny mini skirt, and knee-hi black boots. After removing her clothes they sat on the bed and sipped champagne.

The video had no sound, only the images of the chief with a prostitute or friend. It was very obvious that this was not his wife and that they were not strangers. 'Hawkeye' Lee witnessed their sexual encounters and their shower together. They dressed. Then the chief left the hotel room.

The video again showed another time, Chief entered the hotel room, removed his clothes before he showered, popped open a bottle of champagne, lit some candles and sat on the bed relaxing. Again, there appeared to be a knock on the door. Chief opened the door, and was surprised to have two of his favorite ladies join him, a small framed lady with blonde hair who flashed a warm seductive smile at the lady with the vivid red hair. He pulled them both in the room, kissed them hungrily and they all had sexual relations.

Hawkeye watched intensely. He laughed out loud, "A ménage a trois...Unbelievable!" Usually, Chief Waters left the hotel first, but this time and as he was about to leave, the door opened again and this time a man with a burly build and big black hat that covered his eyes, entered the room. The video revealed him walking directly over to the camera that was recording and it was suddenly unplugged, showing static and obviously ending the recording. The man with the big hat had apparently set the video camera up in the room. "He must be the mysterious MM," concluded Hawkeye. "He is probably the lady's pimp, but I wonder why he would have their sexual acts recorded? Was Chief into pornography and was selling the videos? No," he thought to himself, "Chief would never be that stupid to have his face featured in such a way. Did the pimp come to collect money from the chief for the service the ladies provided? Well, I have the weekend to ponder this video." He laughed again at the thought of the chief with the prostitutes.

Suddenly 'Hawkeye' remembered Chief Skye pulling a few strings to get him in position to be the next chief of police because it was rumored that Chief Waters was a little soft and not well respected as he once was. Instantly the puzzle fell into place. 'Hawkeye' Lee was again proving his brilliance as a detective. The big man with the big hat must have had enough information on the chief to blackmail him. "Perhaps there is more to find out about Chief Waters and his shady friends," he concluded.

CHAPTER 21

Nate entered the Lil Lady Elite restaurant a few minutes early before meeting with former Chief Dan Waters. He was met by one of the waiters that was at work the night he passed out.

"Oh, Mr. Bishop, it is so nice to see you looking so well. You had us all pretty scared."

Nate blushed and shook his extended hand. "Yes all is well today. It was an anxiety attack. No big deal and I am fine. I just have to take it a little easy."

The waiter replied, "It is great to have you back again. Mr. Bishop, Would you like to take your usual seat today? And will Mrs. Bishop be joining you?"

"Actually, I would like to sit in the back for a little privacy. Former Police Chief Waters will be accompanying me for lunch today."

"Oh, yes sir. Please follow me."

Lil Lady Elite was the restaurant known for its delicious food and had the reputation for catering to the pillars of the community and local businesses. Its decor exemplified its name which was both elite as well as elegant. Many secrets were shared within those walls. Every occasion including luncheons, banquets and private parties were hosted for those with refined taste. The atmosphere was always relaxing and comfortable.

As soon as Nate took his seat, the waiter spotted Chief Waters parking his car. "Ahh, Chief Waters has arrived," he announced. Nate's heart sank. "Should I reveal everything? Am I doing the right thing?" he thought. He was hoping to get a few minutes alone to sort out what to tell or what not to tell. "Oh well, let's see how it goes," he muttered under his breath. "After all, he is a friend first, and now the *former* police chief who is retired."

When former Police Chief Dan Waters arrived at Lil Lady Elite to meet Nate, he was feeling fantastic. He sat in his car for a few minutes and reflected back to earlier that morning when he had met with Chief 'Hawkeye' Lee. He felt as if a heavy burden had been lifted from him. His conversation with the new Police Chief Lee, had been like meeting with God and was forgiven of all of his sins. He felt cleansed and renewed. He held nothing back. Chief Waters was grateful that Chief Lee's demeanor had been calm and nonjudgmental. Feeling very comfortable, he told the chief of his devious behavior with the prostitutes. He confided that Big Mc used a video he had of his indiscretions to blackmail him. Chief Lee's demeanor never changed. He thought it would not be wise to make former Chief Waters aware that he already knew, especially after he was able to get the video back into Chief Waters' desk before it was discovered missing.

Hawkeye Lee had asked, "How big is this guy Big Mc in the community?"

Chief Waters thought back to his answer, "Man, he has eyes everywhere in the community so I would say pretty big. After he set me up and threatened to destroy my career and relationship with my wife and children, I did what I was told to do; which was to turn my eyes from all his illegal activities. I am sorry for not being stronger and for being a poor example of a law enforcement agent. I felt the need to come clean this morning because I had an encounter with God last week, and no matter what the consequences I have to face, I had to come clean and tell you everything. I had a copy of the video he took of me and the girls in my desk. Not knowing what to do with it, when I retired, I decided to destroy it. I am so ashamed of it. Thanks so much for listening and if you want to turn me in, I truly understand."

Waters recalled how Chief Lee gazed deeply into his eyes as he spoke. Waters sensed Chief Lee could see the pain and the remorse of his actions and replied, "No, Man, it is not for me to judge you, and now that you have retired, there is no need to do anything, except for me to keep a close eye on you to make sure you are safe. Especially once Big Mc realizes he can't blackmail you anymore. He will have me to deal with now. Just let me know if he contacts you. There is a possibility that he may be the man we have been looking for who has been supplying the east coast with cocaine and marijuana. When I was working undercover in Florida, we got word that a large quantity came into Miami, and by the time the informant told us, it was too late. We believe it was transported in a white van having New York license plates with the word *Paradise* on the driver's door. Our informant told us a few months ago it was headed for a warehouse here in New York .

Chief Waters remembered explicitly the phone call he had received from Chief Skye in Miami just before retiring. He had been asked to brief his officers to be on the lookout for the white van that could have possibly been in his neighborhood. He remained silent, too embarrassed to admit he never informed his officers.

Suddenly, the pieces of the puzzle began to fall into place for Chief Lee as Chief Waters made his incriminating confession." Chief Lee asked, "Do you know Big Mc's real name?"

"Yes, McKenzie Moore," answered Waters.

Immediately Hawkeye Lee knew for sure that those initials MM on the video was none other than McKenzie Moore's, and that he was the man of interest.

Chief 'Hawkeye' Lee asked many questions about Big Mc that morning. Waters answered as best he could, realizing he really did not know much about him at all. He did not know the car he drove, nor did he know where he lived, or the location of his hang out. All he knew was that he did illegal things and the community seemed to respect him and accept him. Now that Chief Lee had Big Mc's full name, he would do what he was trained and paid to do, bring this criminal to justice.

Absorbed and reiterating the conversation he had with Chief Lee, Chief Dan Waters suddenly realized he was five minutes late and Nate was sitting in Lil Lady Elite waiting for him. He quickly turned the car off and joined Nate.

Nate Bishop thanked former Police Chief Dan Waters for meeting him for lunch and got right down to the reason for the meeting.

"Dan, I have known you a long time and I trust and respect your opinion. I am in a situation in which I have to be extremely careful and cautious. So, I need this conversation to be between only the two of us. Are you okay with that?"

"Yes Man, sure. What has gotten you so worried my friend?" Dan asked as he reached out and shook his hand.

Nate poured out his heart and shared about how he stumbled onto the drugs in his warehouse.

Dan asked, "Do you know who is behind it?"

Nate replied, "I believe it is my right hand man, Ricky Clay. At first, I had my doubts, because he has helped get my business back on track, increased the sales, and has just been an awesome asset to my company. But, there is no one else it could be. I spoke to my assistant Teresa, who is in love with Ricky. I believe she is being used by him. She made up certain labels to differentiate his boxes from mine, but it is obvious she had no clue as to what he was really doing. She thought he was sending items to his friends and family and they were sending things back to him to avoid the cost of shipping. The drivers would pick up and drop off my pillows along with his stuff. I spoke with her this morning as well as one of the new hires, Sal Tully. I know I am not a detective but I believe they have absolutely no knowledge at all about what is going on. There are only three of us who have a key to the warehouse as far as I know: Teresa Hayward, Ricky Clay and myself."

Dan was speechless and sat still in disbelief for several minutes. It suddenly occurred to him that the white van with the Paradise logo could be owned by his friend, Nate Bishop. Dan again recalled the conversation he had earlier that morning with Chief Lee when he confessed everything. Not sure of what Nate would think of him, he decided it would not be necessary to tell his old friend of his deplorable life style as police chief.

Dan said, "Well Nate, the best thing to do is to turn this information over to the police to let them stake out your warehouse to see who is behind it. Handling the situation this way will eliminate the possibility of your involvement in drug trafficking and using your business as a cover."

"Yes, thanks a lot for your advice Dan. I really appreciate your insight. I will contact Chief Lee first thing tomorrow morning."

****

The king pin of the drug cartel, Carlos Perez, was beyond angry. Carlos was an extremely dangerous man with a thick Spanish accent who lived in a huge armed and guarded compound in Mexico. His thinning hair showed a hint of gray around the temples which matched his empty steel gray eyes. He was short in stature with a muscular build and spoke with great power even when he whispered. He was quick tempered and very unpredictable. Carlos considered his options very carefully because millions of dollars were at stake. The shipment was delayed, and Big Mc was to blame for the breakdown in the flow, causing a domino effect at the other pick-ups and drop-offs. Some of Carlos's thugs were killed for less than this. Carlos had no sympathy that Big Mc had surgery and was hospitalized.

"I am running a business!" he barked to his main man, Chico. "If Big Mc can make the delivery by Wednesday, all will be well with a minimum loss which will come out of his cut. If not, Big Mc will pay dearly. I can't have weak links!"

****

Big Mc was physically weak and nervous as he left the hospital that Monday morning. It was a bright sun shiny day, but nothing seemed to be bright in Big Mc's life. Still not able to move about very well, and heavily sedated, he decided to take it easy and get as much rest as possible. He had already heard about Carlos' disappointment with him. Well at least it was comforting to know that Ricky had confirmed to meet him on Tuesday morning at the warehouse to get Mr. Carlos' shipment. He knew in spite of his illness, he had to be strong enough to deliver the shipment to the next drop-off in New Jersey. His life was already on the line.

"Tomorrow," he sighed with relief, "Mr. Carlos' goods will be on the way and Ricky and the *BOYS* will be paid. Hopefully Mr. Carlos will forgive me for the breakdown in his operation."

Ricky had no knowledge of where it was going or who would pick it up from Big Mc, nor did he care. He was more concerned with getting his cut for himself and the *BOYS.*

CHAPTER 22

Nate Bishop arrived back at his office around 1:30 PM. He gave the conversation with former Chief Dan Waters a lot of thought. He decided he was going to confront Ricky about the drugs in his warehouse when they would meet at 2:00 PM.

Nate was in deep thought when Ricky tapped on the door and entered, smiling as usual. Startled by his presence, Nate's heart began to pound rapidly. Trying to keep his demeanor calm, he smiled and stood up.

"Yes Ricky. Thanks so much for coming in to talk to me. Have a seat," as he motioned to sit at the conference table facing each other. "So, how are things going Ricky?"

Ricky seemed to beam with pride as he replied, "All is going very well Nate. Since we hired Sal, we are able to make more runs, supplying more of our customers, which is increasing our sales. I was meaning to speak with you about the possibility of expanding to Virginia or Georgia. It would shorten our runs if we had a stop in those states. Right now, Sal is driving straight from here to Florida. If we could get one or two more states along the east coast we may be able to increase our productivity and shorten the drive for Sal. The drop-offs are very punctual and he is making the next connection with no problems. Speaking of Sal, I gave him the week off. He just finished the run to Florida and he and his wife needed some alone time. They've been going through some hard times, so I hope that was okay with you."

Nate made a slight head nod. Ricky continued to talk, trying to impress Nate as he had always done. This time Nate was not bamboozled by what he now knew to be a slick, smooth-talking drug dealer.

"Okay Ricky, I get it now," said Nate. "So, is it that you want to expand my business or *your* business? Which is it?"

Ricky was stunned and caught off guard. He tried to smile but his face felt frozen and stiff.

"Uh, excuse me?" he managed to ask. "What do you mean by that?"

"Well," said Nate, "Before I jump to my own conclusion, I am going to give you a chance to explain what has been going on in my warehouse."

Immediately, Ricky's countenance changed like a chameleon. His eyes bulged and his pupils darkened like steel coal. His nose flared, and veins began to show in his neck and forehead. The transformation itself scared Nate so badly he began to sweat profusely. Ricky pushed back his chair and reached for the gun that he always carried strapped to his ankle. He lunged over the table, yanked Nate by the collar and pressed the barrel of the gun to his head.

Nate yelled, "Ricky! Ricky! What are you doing?" Fear gripped every nerve in his body so badly he could not suppress his urine as it flowed down his legs.

"Okay! Okay!" Ricky yelled back, "You wanna know what I am doing in your warehouse? I am taking care of *my* business while I take care of yours," clenching his teeth. "And you will shut your mouth and pretend we never had this conversation. You continue to run your business and I will continue to run yours and mine and no one will get hurt. Do I make myself clear?" Nate could feel Ricky's hot breath on his neck, and suddenly could not breathe. He reached to loosen his necktie and then everything went black.

At the same time, Teresa was not feeling well and was on her way to the bathroom when she heard loud voices coming from Nate's office. She peered in and was both paralyzed and stunned by the sight of Ricky holding a gun to Nate's head. Teresa stood in disbelief, as if this was a figment of her imagination. Was she dreaming? Was this really happening? Blinking several times, Teresa saw Nate's legs buckle as he collapsed to the floor. Did Ricky shoot Nate? Fearing this was actually real, Teresa quickly stepped back out of view and tiptoed back to her work station trying hard to catch her breath and trying to still her trembling body. Many thoughts were running through her head. "Should I go back and confront Ricky? Call the police? The paramedics? Should I run? Oh God, what do I do?"

Suddenly Teresa heard the sound of heavy footsteps coming down the hall.

"Help! Help! Somebody help! Teresa? Teresa? Call 911! Nate just collapsed in his office. "Hurry! Hurry Up!" Ricky screamed.

Teresa was relieved that he obviously did not see her and was not coming for her. Teresa screamed back, "Okay Ricky I will call 911 and Mrs. Bishop," remembering that

Nate had told her he had also collapsed on Friday evening and had spent the night in the hospital.

"What is going on?" she thought.

Teresa now remembered the warning by Momma King concerning Ricky. Her voice resonated in Teresa's head saying, "Just remember, sometimes people are not always who they appear to be. I just want you to be careful and pay close attention to everything about him."

Teresa rushed down the hall to see Nate and grabbed his desk phone to call 911. "Why didn't Ricky call? He knows I don't have a phone at my workstation," she wondered.

The paramedic arrived within minutes. Recognizing that it was Nate Bishop again, they moved expeditiously, gathering information.

"What happened?" the head paramedic inquired.

Ricky quickly spoke up, "I was going to the office to meet with him. He stood up to greet me and told me he was not feeling well. He reached up to loosen his tie and then collapsed to the floor!"

Teresa thought, "What a blatant lie!"

Nate was still unconscious, and his blood pressure was very elevated along with a rapid heartbeat when they placed him in the ambulance and sped away to Morton Hospital. Mrs. Bishop met the ambulance at the hospital. She quickly assessed Nate's condition and hoped for the best, but prepared for the worst. He looked gravely ill. His face looked drained, grayish and lifeless. She began to cry. She was so afraid of losing Nate. He was her everything. She waited to hear his fate.

CHAPTER 23

Ricky left immediately for the hospital telling Teresa he was going to check on Nate and would meet her later that night for dinner. Teresa sadly nodded her head.

Ricky rushed into the Emergency Room and spotted Lola right away with her head lowered as if she were praying. He had to see what kind of condition Nate was in. Did he regain consciousness and divulge what really happened? He approached Lola with feigned concern and love as he gently touched her shoulder.

"How is he, Mrs. Bishop?" he asked. She lifted her head and smiled, relieved to have someone to sit with her, even if for a moment. She knew how much Nate loved Ricky and what an asset he had been to the company.

"I am still waiting to hear from the doctor. I called his primary doctor, Dr. Drew, who said he would soon be here to see him. I am not sure if he is in there now or not. So Ricky, please tell me exactly what happened?"

Ricky sat down and sighed heavily, repeating his story, "Well, Mrs. Bishop, he told me he wanted to meet with me this afternoon at two o'clock. When I arrived at his office he stood up to greet me and said he didn't feel well. He suddenly grabbed his neck as if he could not breathe and collapsed. I am so sorry Mrs. Bishop."

"Oh, I am so glad you were there and called 911 right away. It could have been worse if you had not reacted so quickly. Thanks so much for having Teresa call me too." Ricky nodded and decided she didn't need to know that it was Teresa who actually called 911. If he could have had his way, he would have left him there to die.

Dr. Drew came out of the Emergency Room. He looked old and worn. His blue eyes which had always sparkled now seemed sad and withdrawn. Lola leaped to her feet, searching his face for answers. She could see that it was not going to be good news.

Ricky stood extending his hand. "I am Ricky Clay, Nate's associate." Dr. Drew nodded and shook his hand. He focused on Lola.

"How is he?" she asked.

Dr. Drew hesitated to speak in the presence of Ricky. "It is okay" she said. "He is like family. You can talk freely," anxious to hear what was going on with Nate.

"Well, Lola. Nate suffered a major stroke. He regained consciousness but he is paralyzed and unable to speak. His eyes are open, but it is a blank stare. I am so sorry Lola," as he reached out and patted her shoulder. "However bad as it may seem, there are a few occasions where stroke victims like Nate do completely recover."

Lola asked, "Can I see him now?"

"Yes, I will go in with you to answer any further questions you may have. In the meantime, I have contacted the best neurologist in the area, Dr. Hughes, to assist me on his case. We will give him the best care possible."

Lola asked Ricky, "Do you want to join us?"

"Uh, no," he replied, "You go on. I will come back later, after I inform everyone at the office and make sure everything is secure."

Lola smiled and said, "Thanks Ricky, I am sure that is exactly what Nate would have wanted also."

CHAPTER 24

It had been a while since Carolyn and Margie's confrontation, but Margie was still having nightmares and not able to sleep. Carolyn's face would still appear taunting her over and over again. Margie thought surely after the punch in her nose Carolyn gave her, and she admitting never to have slept with Sal, that she would be free from the tormenting dreams. Margie decided, enough is enough. She was going to see Madame Zoe, the psychic. Margie always passed Madame Zoe's place of business on her way to work and was always curious about psychics and if they were really able to tell the future. She wanted answers to what the future held for her and how to stop the tormenting dreams.

Tired and struggling to stay awake at her desk, Margie decided to take the rest of the afternoon off. She had plenty of vacation time on the books. Margie worked for Mr. Levine, a reputable attorney with his own law practice. She was his paralegal for the past four years. He was a good employer, very respectable and understanding of his employees. Margie was an excellent employee, always punctual, polite, committed and reliable. She buzzed him in his office and asked if he needed anything, because she was not feeling well and wanted go home and get some rest. Mr. Levine came out of his office looking very concerned.

"Are you okay Margie?" he asked.

"I have been suffering from insomnia lately and I am feeling very fatigued. I need to get some rest," she said.

"Will you be able to get home okay?" he asked.

"Yes, I will be fine. I will see you tomorrow Mr. Levine, and thanks so much," she said taking her purse from her desk and walking toward the door.

"Goodnight and get some rest," he said, turning back to his office.

"Goodnight," she said, exiting the door.

Margie drove directly to Madame Zoe and rang the doorbell. Nervousness had replaced her sleepiness. She was determined to find out what this woman had to say.

Madame Zoe appeared to be in her early fifties, and slightly overweight, with piercing blue eyes. She quickly glanced at Margie from the top of her head to her feet. She noticed that Margie was very attractive and polished. She took note that her nails were nicely manicured, she was well dressed in a navy blue suit, leather pumps and carried a nice Coach designer bag. Madame Zoe understood that anyone who took that much effort with their appearance wanted only the very best for themselves. Madame Zoe conspired, "I must take my time with this one and tap into the *right energy* to convince her that I know her future."

"Please come in," as she stepped back to allow Margie into the foyer.

"Obviously this is the place where she does her business," Margie thought. The house smelled of incense burning, although none was in sight. Margie noticed many candles were burning in the small room off to the right of the large dining area. Madame Zoe pointed to the same small room and told Margie to go in and have a seat. The ceiling and walls were painted black, giving the appearance of the galaxy at night with many celestial stars shining. Although it was dark, the white and silver stars painted on the walls and ceiling appeared to illuminate the room. The candles burning seemed to be alluring and created an ambience of comfort and relaxation. In the center of the room was a card table with two chairs facing each other and a large crystal ball in the center of the table. Margie graciously accepted the invitation and sat down, wondering what would happen next. Madame Zoe smiled and gazed deeply into her eyes as she sat across from her.

"I am Madame Zoe and I see you are very troubled about certain things going on in your life," as she noticed the discoloration and bags under Margie's eyes. She took advantage of that and said, "You are losing sleep and not resting well."

Margie looked surprised and nodded her head slightly.

"I see many things concerning your life, but we must first talk of how my service works. I will tell you as much as the *spirits* will allow me to tell you today for a fee of $50.00. Could you pay this now?"

"Ahh, sure," Margie said, reaching for her pocketbook, curious now than ever to hear more. Madame Zoe quickly took the crisp fifty dollar bill and tucked it in her brassiere.

"Okay, now we must begin. Please place your hands in mine around the crystal ball and tell me your name and your date of birth."

As Margie placed her hand in hers, Madame Zoe noticed she wore no wedding ring. This observation told her that Margie was probably not married. Madame Zoe explained that they must stay hand in hand for the session so the *spirits* can channel the information to her correctly. Margie stated her name and birth date in a robotic voice with her eyes closed. This was the beginning of weekly visits to Madame Zoe. The dreams of Carolyn tormenting her stopped coincidently three days after her visits to Madame Zoe, but the shame and embarrassment were still gnawing away at her conscience. How could she get rid of the shame? She never felt ashamed before when she had inappropriate relations with other married men. Why now?

Before long, Margie could not make a decision without first conferring with Madame Zoe. Madame Zoe was right as many times as she was wrong about predicting Margie's future, but Margie felt compelled to continue allowing Madame Zoe to have dominance over her life, sometimes paying her as much as five hundred dollars a month. Margie was convinced that Madame Zoe was removing evil from around her as well as the pain of her childhood, which had eventually caused her to become promiscuous as an adult. She thought that Madame Zoe had power over her future. In spite of many readings including the tarot cards and séances, Margie still felt like she was in a heavy cloud and that something was sucking the very life from her. She was drained and empty.

CHAPTER 25

Feeling overwhelmed and frustrated at work, Margie went into the bathroom and began weeping uncontrollably. What was wrong with her? Was she having some sort of breakdown? Madame Zoe never predicted this. Why was she continuing to feel so down and depressed most of the time?

Shironi Rawlson had worked for Mr. Levine for the past eight years and was the nurturing mother type whom everyone loved. Shironi was in her late forties and strikingly beautiful. She was always upbeat and consistently seemed to be in a good mood. She was the *go to* person if there was a problem, whether work related or socially. She was a devout Christian after being delivered ten years ago from drugs and the lifestyle of being a *call girl*. She opened the bathroom door and was surprised to see Margie crying hysterically.

"Oh, Honey, what's wrong?" as she moved in to put her arms around Margie.

"I am okay" Margie replied, only because she did not know what to say was wrong.

"Well, no matter what you are experiencing, Jesus loves you and He has a plan and a purpose for your life. There is purpose in your pain," Shironi said.

Margie did not want to be rude, but she really did not want to hear anything about Jesus and His love for her.

"Where was He when I was being abused mentally, verbally, and sexually most of my life by different men?" she thought. Margie's heart had grown hard toward God and to committed relationships. She was determined to use all men before they used her.

Shironi continued to tell her about Jesus and how He changed her life. "He is bigger than the pain you are feeling now if you will just give it to Him, Margie. He will take your pain and give you peace." Margie did not understand what Shironi was saying but there was something about her voice and demeanor that was very soothing and convincing. Shironi continued on and asked if she could pray for her. Margie nodded her head in agreement.

Shironi prayed, "*Dear God in heaven, You are my best friend and my only hope, which is why I know I can always talk to You about everything. So God, in the Name of Your Son, Jesus Christ, I ask You to take away Margie's pain, both past and present. Please show her how much You love her and let her experience Your peace and joy that only You can give her. Please draw her to You by Your Holy Spirit. Thank you so much Father God. In the Name of Jesus. I love you. Amen."*

Margie was immediately amazed at how calm she began to feel. It was as if heavy weights were being lifted from her body. She smiled and thanked Shironi.

"I am here anytime you need me," Shironi replied. "In fact, tomorrow night we are having our Young Adults Sharing the Power program at our church. Would you please come as my special guest?"

"Yes," without hesitation Margie replied, not sure why she answered so quickly or if she really wanted to go.

"I would love to introduce you to my pastor, Pastor W. Dale Sherman, and some of the young adults like yourself."

"What is the name of your church?" Margie asked.

"It is the Light of Love located on the corner of Prospect and Newfoundland Street," Shironi answered.

"Oh, yes, I know where it is," Margie said looking in the mirror to adjust her long eyelashes.

"Great! It starts at 7:30 PM. Would you like me to pick you up?" asked Shironi.

"No," Margie said, "I will meet you there. Thank you so much Shironi. I really do feel surprisingly so much better."

Shironi smiled and gave her a big hug. Margie took another look in the mirror and freshened up her makeup around her eyes and said, "Okay I will see you tomorrow," as she walked out the door.

CHAPTER 26

Ricky arrived at the hospital a little before 5 PM that evening to check on Nate's status. Lola was sitting in a chair facing Nate with her back turned away from the door. She did not see Ricky as he entered the room. Although it appeared that Nate's eyes were fixated and staring off into space, he suddenly showed signs of awareness. Unable to speak, his eyes began to flutter and swell up with tears as Ricky said hello to Lola.

"How is he doing?" Ricky spoke out."

Lola, surprised to see Nate's reaction, was extremely excited as she spun around to greet Ricky.

"Well, he definitely recognizes you Ricky. Look! He is crying! He is so happy you are here. I will be right back. I am going to get his nurse!" Lola exclaimed, rushing toward the door.

Alone with Nate, Ricky looked intensely into his face.

Ricky sneered sarcastically, "Now look what happened. Well at least while you are here, I don't have to worry about you doing something that you will regret as long as you can't talk. My operation will continue, and I will continue to help you and your business. Nate, just so you know, I was coming back here to finish you off, but since you can't speak and are no longer a threat, I will let Lola hold on to the hope that you are at least still alive. It is just a matter of time as you know. Your days are almost over, Ol' Man. I will check on you every day, just to make sure you are *not* getting better."

Nate's eyes fluttered more and more rapidly, as tears streamed down his face.

Lola arrived quickly with his nurse, Veronica. She observed the change and made notes on his medical chart.

"Ms. Bishop, are you aware that Dr. Hughes, his neurologist, will be here tomorrow to evaluate him?"

"Yes," Lola replied.

Veronica continued to explain, "This is the early stages of his stroke and it can go in many different directions. It is too early to tell for sure. As you know, Dr. Hughes is the best in the field. Nate will have the best of care."

Ricky listened intently to their conversation and at the appropriate time, he interrupted them to tell Mrs. Bishop that he was leaving, because he promised to meet Teresa for dinner.

"I will come back to check on Nate tomorrow." He paused as he turned back and said, "Mrs. Bishop, is there anything I can do for you? Do you need anything...anything at all?"

Mrs. Bishop smiled warmly, and gave him a big hug and reassured him she was fine and she was going to stay at the hospital that night in case there was a change. "I just want to be close to Nate," she whispered.

Ricky smiled, nodding his head.

"Yes, of course, I totally understand," he said as he rubbed her shoulder. "I hope he gets better, but I don't want you to worry about Paradise Pillows. I have everything under control. So focus all your energy on Nate."

Mrs. Bishop smiled and thanked him graciously for his dedication and commitment to Nate. Turning back to look at him, Nate's eyes continued to flutter as tears soaked his face.

CHAPTER 27

Teresa was still trying to understand what actually happened with Nate and Ricky that day. She sat trying to figure out everything that transpired, but nothing made any sense. Teresa was a little nervous but assured herself that there was a logical explanation; but "Why did Ricky have a gun? Why did he threaten Nate with it?" she queried. It all just seemed so out of character for Ricky. He loved Nate and Nate loved him. In fact, everyone loved Ricky at Paradise.

Teresa called Ms. King to ask if Jamie could have dinner with her and possibly spend the night because she did not want to talk in front of Jamie. Ms. King eagerly agreed. She loved Jamie and enjoyed doing different things with him. She loved telling him Bible stories and how much Jesus loves him.

Teresa met Ricky at Lil Lady Elite around 6 PM. He smiled as he stepped out of the car and opened the door for her. She tried to smile, but her face felt stiff.

Ricky asked, "Where's Jamie?"

"Oh, I left him with Momma King tonight. I was hoping if it was not too late, after dinner we could go to the hospital to see Nate. How was he doing?" she asked.

"Not good Teresa. He is all messed up," he replied, as they walked into the restaurant.

The atmosphere was buzzing with the news of Nate Bishop being hospitalized. Several people inquired about Nate's condition when they recognized Teresa and Ricky walking in.

"He appears to have suffered a major stroke. He's paralyzed and unable to speak," Ricky responded with such feigned pity.

Teresa shuddered just thinking of Nate's fate, and what might happen to Paradise Pillows made her tremble. She decided to go see Nate for herself first thing the next morning because it would probably be too late that night.

The hostess greeted them and sat them in the back of the now crowded restaurant.

Ricky was his smooth slick self. He noticed Teresa was not as talkative as usual.

"Teresa, are you okay?" he asked.

"Yes, I am okay, but could you tell me what happened today in Nate's office? I thought he was better because he recently was hospitalized for an anxiety attack over the weekend. He was kept overnight and released. He assured me he was doing better and was looking forward to meeting with you earlier today. So what happened?" she asked.

When Teresa was upset, she had a tendency to ask many questions before they could be answered. Ricky reached across the table to hold her hands and looked deeply into her eyes. "Teresa, I know it has been a very upsetting day with all that you have been through, but everything is going to be okay. Mrs. Bishop wants us to make sure we run the company just as Nate would. I assured her we will. I need you to be strong and work with me to make things go well. Nate and Lola are counting on us. Okay?"

"Ricky, what happened today with Nate?" she asked again in an accusatory tone.

"What do you mean Teresa?" he asked. "I don't know. I went into the office and he stood up to loosen his tie as if he were not getting enough air, and then suddenly he passed out," he lied. "You are worried about Nate and I am too. I understand you are concerned but it will be okay Teresa. Everything is going to work out. I am glad you didn't bring Jamie tonight. He does not need to know about this, okay?" he said, trying to shift the attention to Jamie.

Teresa knew in her heart, he was lying and with such ease. It was scary.

"Who is this monster that I have fallen in love with? Why is he lying? I think I will play it cool until I can figure out exactly what he is up to." she thought.

Teresa had a flashback of Nate questioning her about the labels she made for Ricky marked *BOYS*. Could this have something to do with Nate being threatened? Suddenly, there was Momma King's voice in her head warning her about Ricky.

Teresa smiled and shook her head in agreement, "Yes, Ricky you are right. I am just overly worried."

I must not let him know I saw him today with a gun to Nate's head," she thought. *"Oh God, what do I do? Are Jamie and I in danger? Please God, I need your help!"*

Teresa was trying to understand what had transpired earlier, while Ricky was thinking about meeting Big Mc the next morning to make the score of a lifetime. He and the *BOYS* would be splitting the biggest drug deal ever... three and a half million dollars! He was elated and more confident than ever now that Nate was out of the way. He was confident that he could convince Mrs. Bishop to allow him to run the business upon Nate's demise.

Ricky focused on Teresa and noticed she was in deep thought and still picking at her food.

"Hey Babe, it has been a long day. Let's make it an early night. Would you like to take your food home?" he asked.

Teresa did not seem to hear him. Ricky gently touched her hand to get her attention. Teresa's big brown eyes that once sparkled with so much life were now dim and sad.

"Yeah, sure Ricky," she said trying to muster a smile. Ricky signaled the waiter, paid the bill and escorted Teresa to her car. He gave her a light kiss on her forehead. "Goodnight Teresa, I will check on you later," he said.

Teresa nodded.

CHAPTER 28

News of Nate Bishop's circumstance traveled quickly in the close knit community. Former Police Chief Waters was stunned and in disbelief. He had just had lunch with him a few hours earlier. He left his home immediately to go check on him. The former Police Chief prayed all the way to the hospital, asking God if he should divulge the information that Nate had shared with him to Mrs. Bishop. Should he call Police Chief Lee to tell what Nate had confided in him?

Mrs. Bishop was fussing over Nate making sure he was comfortable in his private room. They had just transferred him to the VIP wing of the hospital. She heard a light knock on the door and quickly walked over and opened it. Surprised to see Chief Waters, she motioned him in and thanked him for coming. Nate's eyes moved and focused on Chief Waters as he approached the bed. Mrs. Bishop noticed his eyes were no longer fixated or fluttering.

"I came as soon as I heard, Lola. How is he doing?" he asked very softly with great concern.

"Well, he suffered a stroke and he is paralyzed and unable to speak. But I just noticed when he heard your voice, his eyes focused in on you. It appears he knows you are here. Dr. Hughes, his neurologist will be here tomorrow to evaluate his condition. He is the best in the field, according to Dr. Drew. He has seen patients such as Nate completely recover." As Lola was speaking, she suddenly realized that Nate was now looking at her. She was so excited and told Chief Waters she was going to get the nurse. His eyes were no longer fluttering or fixated.

Chief Waters was happy to be in the room alone with Nate. Lola rushed out of the room and Chief Waters took advantage of this opportunity to see if he could somehow communicate with Nate. He stood by his bedside and looked Nate squarely in the face. Nate's eyes focused squarely on him.

"Nate, I need to know what I should do with the information you told me earlier today. If you can hear me and understand what I am saying can you blink your eyes?" Nate immediately blinked his eyes.

Chief gave him a big smile and said, "Just to make sure you are hearing me, will you blink your eyes two times?"

Nate immediately blinked two times.

"Oh, that is great Buddy," Chief smiled again. "Now, should I tell Lola what you shared with me today?"

Nate stared deeply into his eyes. He did not blink.

"Okay, you do not want me to tell Lola right. Blink now if that is right."

Nate blinked.

"Okay, thanks Buddy I will keep that from her for now, but you've got to get better. We can't let Ricky get away with this. You told me today that you were going to speak to Police Chief Lee about this. Did you speak with him yet?"

Nate stared into his eyes.

"Do you want me to tell him what you told me?"

Nate blinked.

"Okay, I will inform him this evening. Is that okay?"

Nate blinked.

"Nate, I want you to know something that happened to me a few months ago, while I was Chief of Police. I did some things that I am not proud of, which is why I had to see the new Chief of Police today. Confession is good for the soul. I was not able to sleep some nights and the guilt was overwhelming. I would cry out to God and ask for forgiveness. I don't want to talk about what I did right now, but I want to tell you what God did. He heard my cry, forgave me, and came into my life! He took away the guilt and shame and healed my heart! I have never felt so free and so alive in my life! I feel so close to God now and I am reading the Bible every day. I know Jesus died on the Cross, so we can be free of our sins and have a relationship with God. Nate would you like Jesus to come into your heart?"

Nate blinked his eyes.

"Okay," Chief said, "Let's pray. You pray in your heart and I will pray out loud and ask Jesus to come into your heart." Nate closed his eyes. Chief prayed with such simplicity and childlike faith.

"Dear God, I come to You in the Name of Jesus. Please go into Nate's heart just like You came into mine and washed away all of my sins. God, please heal him and

restore his life. Thank You Father and I believe You will do it for Your Glory and Honor. In the Name of Your Son Jesus. Amen."

Nate and Chief opened their eyes just as Lola opened the door with the nurse.

"Perfect timing," thought Chief Waters.

CHAPTER 29

Frustrated and confused, Teresa did not want to go home after dinner. She said good night to Ricky and headed right to Momma King's house. She needed to talk to someone. She felt overwhelmed with all the events of the day. Many things were unnerving and unsettled in her mind.

Momma King was surprised and happy to see Teresa.

"Teresa is everything okay?" Momma King inquired.

"Well actually I wanted to talk to you. Is Jamie in bed?" Teresa asked.

"Oh, yes. I put him to bed about an hour ago. What's wrong Sweetie?" Momma King asked while motioning her to the kitchen. "I just put on some hot water. Let's have a cup of tea and talk about what is troubling you."

Teresa smiled and followed her into the kitchen. She sat silently at the table as she watched Momma King hastily prepare the tea. Ms. King began to pray within herself, asking God to give her wisdom and discernment to help Teresa.

Ms. King sat down and placed the hot cup of tea in front of Teresa. She wrapped her hands around the cup as though to warm her hands. Teresa looked deeply troubled as she stared into the cup of tea.

"Momma King, something terrible happened today and I don't know what to do," she blurted.

"What happened Sweetie?" Momma King asked.

"It's Nate Bishop! He is in the hospital. He suffered a bad stroke today. He is paralyzed and can't speak and Ricky...(her voice trailed off, suddenly having second thoughts about telling what she saw earlier)...and Momma King, I am so afraid for him. He looked gravely ill. Will you pray for him?" she implored.

"Of course. Now don't you worry. We will go to see him tomorrow, after Jamie goes to school. I will pray for him and lay hands on him. I believe there is nothing too hard for God. He is a mighty healer and deliverer. In the Bible, the 16th chapter of Mark verses 17 and 18, Jesus said, *"And these signs shall follow them that believe; In My Name they shall cast out devils; they shall speak with new tongues; they shall take up serpents; and if they drink any deadly thing, it shall not hurt them; they shall lay hands on the sick, and they shall recover."* Momma King moved over to Teresa and said, "We will go pray for Nate tomorrow, but may I pray with you now?" Teresa reflected back to the many times Jamie told stories of Momma King praying for him and how he always felt warm and tingly. Would she feel warm and tingly, she wondered.

"Sure Momma King. Thank you."

"Teresa, before I pray for you, did you know that God thought of you before you were in your mother's womb, and He has a plan and a purpose for your life? Sometimes there are a lot of painful things that may happen in life that seem so unfair. It is those times that if God did not allow the life-altering circumstances, we would never come to know the love of God and experience His Loving Grace. There are benefits in the pain and suffering experiences. It helps us to learn important lessons in life. It teaches us courage and how to help comfort others who have had similar experiences. Pain and suffering can shape our character. It is like taking a terrible tasting medicine and even though it tastes badly, it produces good results. We are like gold, so precious to

God, but to make the gold the best it can be, it must be refined by fire. The fire heats the gold and burns away all the impurities. Trials and tribulations are character builders and facilitate us to seek God and become more like Him. Think about the process of the olives. They have to be crushed or pressed until the oil is produced, so it can be used. Sometimes, before God can use us the way He desires, we must be broken and humbled. No matter what the experiences are, the beautiful thing is that Jesus makes it possible for us to endure the hardships. He promises to always be with us. Would you like Jesus to come into your heart to fulfill the plan and the purpose He has for your life?" asked Momma King.

Teresa simply nodded her head, surrendering to the love-filled words of hope and salvation.

"Okay, first I would like to anoint you with oil. It represents a point of contact and an impartation of the Holy Spirit upon your life. I want to anoint your head. Is that okay Teresa?"

Again, Teresa nodded her head and closed her eyes. Momma King anointed her head by making the sign of the cross with oil on her forehead. It smelled of frankincense and myrrh, which had a very pleasant but distinct odor.

Momma King told Teresa to repeat after her. Teresa repeated what Momma King called the 'Sinner's Prayer'. The prayer consisted of acknowledging Jesus as the Son of God, who died on the Cross for her sins, asking for forgiveness, and lastly receiving Him into her heart. When they finished, Momma King began to rejoice and shouted, "Halleluiah! over and over again." Teresa did not know what to expect but continued to keep her eyes closed.

Momma King hugged her and began to pray a more intense prayer. *"Father, I know You love Teresa, and You have a plan and purpose for her life. Reveal Your plan to her Father. Reveal to her the very thoughts You have toward her. She is a good mother to Jamie and tries to be a good person, but she needs You as her personal Savior. Redeem her and Jamie. I ask You to protect them from all hurt, harm and danger. Cover them both with Your precious blood and fill her with Your Spirit that she may be able to understand Your Words of Truth. Create in her a clean heart and renew a right Spirit within her. Fill her with a hunger as never before for You and Your righteousness. And Father God, remember Nate Bishop and his affliction and touch his body and restore him in Jesus Name. Father, You have said in Your Word in Isaiah 53:4-5: 'Surely, Jesus has borne our griefs, and carried our*

sorrows: yet we did esteem Him stricken, smitten of God, and afflicted. But He was wounded for our transgressions, He was bruised for our iniquities: the chastisement of our peace was upon Him; and with His stripes we are healed.'
I decree and declare healing for Nate Bishop in Your Name Jesus. Amen!"

Teresa was shaking uncontrollably as the Peace of God flooded her soul and bubbled over into tears and unspeakable joy. She began shouting, "Thank you Jesus! Thank you Jesus!" Over and over again. Momma King joined in and continued to praise and thank God. Teresa felt a warmth and a tingling sensation all over her body, just as Jamie had said. Suddenly she was speaking in a language she had never heard before, nor did she understand what she was saying. The more she spoke in the unknown tongues, the deeper the Peace of God filled her soul, the more the tears rolled down her face, and the stress of the day lifted completely. They rejoiced and praised God for over an hour!

They both felt refreshed and renewed and at the same time felt exhausted and ready for bed. It was getting late so Momma King suggested Teresa spend the night, which she gladly accepted.

Just as Teresa was heading for bed, Momma King said, "We are having our Young Adults Sharing the Power Celebration tomorrow night at church. I would love for you and Jamie to come as my special guests. I have told so many there about you and Jamie. Pastor Sherman would love to meet you too."

Teresa thought, "How could I possibly say no to her, even if I wanted to?"

She responded, "Yes, and thanks so much for inviting us. Jamie always said he wanted to go to church with you. He will be thrilled! Thank you! And Momma King, thank you for everything and especially that prayer for me and Jamie. I feel so beautiful inside, like my soul has been washed clean." Teresa exclaimed. "I know something wonderful happened when I started speaking in a language I didn't know. Can you explain what happened to me?"

"Sure thing my child. You were filled with the Holy Spirit of God and the evidence that it happened was you spoke with an unknown tongue. There is a Bible on the night stand in the room you will be sleeping in. Read all about it in Acts the second chapter. We can discuss it later if you don't understand." Momma King smiled and added,

"To God be the Glory for the things He has done! Jesus loves you and has a plan and a purpose for your life. Now that you have accepted Him into your life, He can now teach you His ways and direct your life so His purpose can be fulfilled."

"Thank you Momma King," she squealed in excitement.

Teresa started again for bed and Momma King said, "Oh yes, Teresa one more thing. I know there is more to the story about what happened today that you have not shared with me. Perhaps we can talk about it tomorrow. I love you and good night."

Teresa was stunned. "Did God tell her?" Turning back to face her, Teresa smiled and replied. "Yes, tomorrow. Thank you Momma King. I feel so much better just knowing you are here for me and Jamie. I love you too. Good night."

Even though Teresa became born-again and felt the Peace of God, she did not want to admit that Ricky had frightened her badly. She was so grateful she did not have to go home to an empty house alone tonight. She had a lot to think about before morning.

"Should I tell Momma King everything? If I tell her about the gun, will she call the police on Ricky? What should I do when I see Ricky tomorrow at work? Well, first things first," she thought. "I will pray. *God, now that I have You in my heart, please help me and give me wisdom. Show me what I need to know about Ricky and his true character. And thank You for Momma King being so kind and a part of our lives. Please continue to bless her and keep her under Your protection. And please Father, In Jesus name, heal Nate and comfort Mrs. Bishop. Thank You Jesus for coming into my life and letting me feel Your presence. Amen.*"

CHAPTER 30

Ring. Ring.

"Hello? Chief Lee? It is Dan Waters."

"Yes, Dan. How can I help you?" the chief replied.

"Sorry to bother you at home Chief, but I just left Morton Hospital visiting Nate Bishop, the owner of Paradise Pillows Corporation. He suffered a major stroke this afternoon. He is paralyzed and unable to speak. I had lunch with him earlier today and he told me some things that I think you need to know. Is it okay to speak to you now?" Dan asked.

'Yes, it's fine," Chief Lee replied.

"Let me get my pad," shifting the phone to his left ear. "Okay, I am ready now," he said grabbing his pad and pen.

Dan began, "Nate said he stumbled across marijuana and cocaine stored in boxes in his warehouse, instead of pillows. He was very concerned and wanted advice as to how to handle the situation. He thinks his maintenance man, Ricky Clay may be responsible for drug trafficking. Nate was going to call you, but now he has suffered the stroke and is unable to speak."

"Okay, thank you Dan. I am on it. Thanks for the heads up. Oh, by the way, do you know if Big Mc and Ricky Clay are connected in any way?" Chief inquired.

"I don't know for sure, but there is a strong possibility. I do know Big Mc has a lot of thugs working for him," Dan said.

"Okay, I appreciate the information. I will say a prayer for Nate. It does not make sense to go to the hospital to question him about his findings in his condition. So give him my best regards, will you?" Chief Lee said. He had not had the pleasure of meeting Nate since he relocated. Chief Lee knew of his well respected reputation and established corporation.

"Well, I found a way to communicate with him. He can answer your questions by blinking, but could you hold off a bit because he does not want his wife to know about the drugs in the warehouse yet. She is like a permanent fixture at his bedside and he does not want her to worry," said Dan.

"Okay, I will investigate and thanks so much again." Chief Lee said.

"Okay, thank you," Dan said. "Have a good night."

"Good night and keep in touch," Chief Lee replied.

Chief Lee called four of his top undercover agents to begin a stakeout of the warehouse starting at 5AM that morning. Agent Marco and Agent Haddon were briefed and advised that any vehicle leaving the warehouse was to be tailed by the two undercover detectives waiting at the end of the street. They were to stay put and watch everyone and everything coming and going from Paradise Pillows and radio back any activity.

"Take pictures of license plates, drivers, and receivers if possible, but do not compromise this stakeout! We want all involved in this cartel! And keep me posted!" Chief ordered.

****

Big Mc was extremely sore from the gall bladder operation. But it did not matter how he felt. He knew if he did not deliver the shipment as planned, his life was in jeopardy. It was necessary to get to the mausoleum which was just on the outskirts of town. He purchased the mausoleum a few years earlier for himself upon his demise. While waiting for that day, Big Mc used it to hide drugs, guns and the three and a half million dollars from Mr. Carlos Perez, the king pin of the cartel. Big Mc had the money packed neatly in three large duffel bags. The money was to pay Ricky and the *BOYS* when he picked up the shipment at 6 AM.

Big Mc took extra care when he arose at 4:30 AM that Tuesday morning to pick up the shipment. He remembered the duffel bags were heavy and his doctor had advised him not to lift anything heavy for a couple of weeks. He wrapped his stomach very tightly to keep the stitches in place and from pulling. Big Mc drove the big blue commercial van that he always used in the transport to the next hub. He arrived at the warehouse at 6 AM as instructed. Ricky was waiting and so were the two unseen undercover agents. They had camouflaged themselves in a way so they could see every movement at the warehouse. Ricky arrived at 5:45 AM and waited inside the warehouse until Big Mc pulled in. Big Mc backed the van up to the warehouse and opened up the rear doors to the van. Ricky came out, greeted Big Mc, and quickly loaded the shipment into the van.

Big Mc opened the passenger side of the van and gave Ricky two of the large duffel bags. As he reached for the third bag, he suddenly fell to his knees in excruciating pain while holding his stomach. He thought something ripped on the inside of his stomach. He dropped the bag, exposing a large sum of money. Ricky helped him get up and quickly shoved the money back into the bag and placed it in the trunk of his Chevy.

Agent Marco and Haddon watched closely and took numerous pictures of everything, including Big Mc's fall. They took pictures of Ricky's car and Big Mc's van, their license plates, the boxes labeled Paradise Pillows *BOYS,* as well as the duffel bags.

The highly magnified cameras they used worked like binoculars, enabling them to see everything very clearly. Being careful not to be noticed, they radioed in for the tail car to get into position to follow the blue commercial van. They advised the chief of the large sum of money in duffel bags in the trunk of the black and gold Chevy along with the license plate number.

"You alright man?" asked Ricky.

Big Mc whispered, "Yeah Man, just help me get to the van." Ricky steadied Big Mc as he helped him into the van.

"I can make it to the next drop. It is only about an hour drive to New Jersey for the drop-off. I can make it," trying to reassure himself.

"Okay, Man, take it nice and easy, okay?" Ricky warned.

"Yeah Man thanks," as he drove off.

The unmarked police car followed at a distance...

CHAPTER 31

The Angel of the Lord shook Ms. King and awakened her at 5 AM. She was very aware of His presence in her bedroom but could not see Him. She was overwhelmed with great joy and peace just as she remembered the night Jesus rocked her to sleep. While she was reliving the moment, she suddenly heard a voice that seemed to speak from within her and around her simultaneously.

"My daughter, I have need of thee today. Arise and shine for the Glory of the Lord has risen upon you this day. You will do great things in My Name. You are commissioned this day to do My Will and signs and wonders shall follow you because you believe in Me. I am well pleased, My daughter. I am the Lord thy God, Jehovah El Shaddai is My Name."

Ms. King was so grateful and humbled that God would speak to her in such a manner. She rolled out of bed and lay prostrate on the bedroom floor. She wept softly praising and thanking God for His kindness toward her. She felt so unworthy of such a visitation and experience. She remained in the same position in the presence of God until she heard a soft tapping on her door. Ms. King slowly sat up and crawled back into her bed.

"Yes," she answered.

"Momma King, it is 7:30 AM and I am leaving for work now. I will put Jamie on the bus, okay?" Teresa said softly.

"Yes, my dear, I did not realize the time. I will stop by your office around nine o'clock and we can go to the hospital to see Nate Bishop. Is that a good time for you?" Momma King gently inquired, still feeling the awesome presence of God.

"Yes, that will be perfect. I will see you then, okay?"

"Give Jamie a kiss for me and you guys be safe."

"Okay, see you later." Teresa said.

Teresa arrived at work as usual around 8 AM. She was surprised to see Ricky already busy at work in the warehouse.

"What is he doing here so early? What is he up to?" she questioned herself.

Ricky noticed Teresa had arrived just as she was getting out of her car. He smiled and waved at her. Teresa waved back and headed to the office. She had a few things to take care of before going to the hospital. She typed out a few memos to inform the department heads regarding Nate's condition and that Paradise Pillows would be business as usual until further notice. Teresa had promised to keep everyone informed and encouraged everyone to keep Nate in their prayers.

Ricky seemed to be joyful and strangely happy when he entered the office and spoke to Teresa. Teresa tried to smile but everything about a smile and being happy was missing from her face. Ricky noticed Teresa's reaction, and quickly tried to reassure her.

"I know you are very concerned about Nate, but everything will be okay. He is counting on you and me to keep Paradise up and running smoothly. Mrs. Bishop is counting on us as well. She told me that yesterday and I assured her that we would not let them down. So I need you to be strong Teresa, okay?" Rick said gently. He put his arms around her and hugged her tightly. For a moment, Teresa believed he was sincere and felt herself falling for his lies and deceit again.

"Oh, Teresa, you are trembling. Are you okay?"

"Yes, I am fine," trying to free herself from his hold as she pulled backward. She was trying very hard not to appear afraid of Ricky. She was determined to find out exactly what he was up to while that image of him with a gun to Nate's head made her feel sick with fear.

"Oh," Ricky said, "I forgot to tell you I gave Sal the week off. He took his wife to the Poconos to get reacquainted. When things return to normal around here, I would like to take you there. Would you like to go? Jamie can stay with Ms. King and it can be just the two of us. It is long overdue and you are so deserving. What do you say Teresa?"

Trying hard to avoid his eyes, Teresa turned and walked over to her work station.

"I think that is a great idea Ricky. It is just not the right time with so much going on with Nate. Let's plan it after Nate gets well and is back to work. After all, you said he is counting on us to hold everything together right?" Teresa turned to face Ricky and managed to give a convincing smile.

"Yeah, sure Teresa, let's wait," Ricky said. While he thought to himself, "Nate is never going to return to Paradise Pillows. He is a dead man the next opportunity I am alone with him. I will take care of Mrs. Bishop and convince her to keep the business going and she will allow me to run the corporation. If not, she will be eliminated as well. We can become multimillionaires very quickly. This is the perfect set up and nothing is going to stop me and the *BOYS* connection."

"Oh, by the way," Ricky remembered, "I have to go to the bank around noon today, so I may be out for a while because I am also going to check on Nate before I return back here. So, I will see you later this evening. Put on something really nice because two of my buddies are flying in this evening and I want them to meet my girl," he announced smiling proudly.

"Oh Ricky, I am sorry I forgot to tell you, but I promised Momma King I would go to church with her tonight," she said.

"Church?" Ricky said with unbelief. "You are kidding, right?"

"No not at all. Jamie and I are going as her special guests. They are having their Young Adults Share the Power Celebration. I'm sure you and your friends can come with us if you like," she encouraged.

"Well, no thank you. I have heard a lot about Pastor Sherman's church. That is where Ms. King goes right?"

"Yes, how did you hear about the church?" she asked.

"A long time ago, I met this man who went to that church. He was a big gangster and went to church from time to time because he said it made him feel better. He was a really bad dude and wanted to change his lifestyle but he was in too deep and could not walk away. He told me there is something different about that church and Pastor Sherman."

"Really? And who might that be?" she asked, gazing into his eyes.

"His name is not important and you would not know him anyway," he resisted.

"So, if I won't know who he is then what is the big deal of saying his name," she said agitatedly.

"Hey Babe, it is no big deal, no need to get upset. His name is McKenzie Moore. See, you don't know him right?" Ricky deliberately did not give his street name of Big Mc as he is known in the community.

"No, you are right, I don't know him. I am looking forward to seeing what this church is all about. Are you sure you and your friends don't want to come?" she asked.

Just as Ricky was about to answer, the front office door opened. They both turned to see who it was coming in. Ms. King stepped inside and smiled warmly at Teresa and Ricky.

"Good morning," she said.

"Oh, Momma King, I did not realize the time. It is 9 o'clock already? I will be ready to leave as soon as I get my purse. Oh, Ricky I forgot to tell you we were going to the hospital to see Nate. I will be back before noon and you can do your banking." Ricky looked stunned and speechless as he stood gazing at Ms. King. He thought, "Teresa seems different somehow. She never mentioned that she and Ms. King were going to church together and now they are going to the hospital. She always shared everything with me."

Leaving Ricky and Ms. King together in the waiting area, Teresa went to get her purse. Ms. King continued to smile at Ricky. "You seemed surprised. Is everything okay?" she asked.

"Yes, I did not know that you knew Nate Bishop."

Still smiling, Ms. King said, "You are right, I don't know Nate, but you don't have to know a person to pray for them. I pray for you too."

Ricky was relieved when Teresa came back with her purse. He never felt comfortable in the presence of Ms. King and certainly did not know how to respond when she told him she prayed for him too. It felt as if she could see deep into his dark soul and knew things about him that he never wanted to divulge to anyone. He never understood why, but he knew it was real and not a figment of his imagination. "Why am I suddenly surrounded by people talking about God to me," he considered. "First, Sal telling me about his transformation and my heart was actually feeling compassion for the first time. Then, Big Mc telling me how he goes to church sometimes because it makes him feel better. Teresa inviting me to go to church with her, and now Ms. King telling me she is praying for me. Oh well," he thought, "It doesn't matter because in a few hours my life will be so changed that even God will not recognize me," as he thought of the three and a half million dollars in the trunk of his car.

"Okay, I will see you later," Ricky yelled as they walked out the door.

"I will be back soon," Teresa shouted back. Ms. King continued to smile and nodded her head in a way as if to say good-bye.

CHAPTER 32

The two undercover detectives, Agents Marco and Haddon radioed Chief Lee that Ricky Clay was the owner of the black and gold Chevy. Agent Marco reported, "Two ladies are now leaving Paradise and the male subject is still in the building. Should we follow them or call for another tail?"

"No, stay put and follow the money. Look for any opportunity to seize the money without being seen," Chief Lee radioed back to the detectives. "Do not make any attempt to arrest our suspect. He is our bait."

Agent Marco suddenly had a brilliant idea. "Hey Chief, how about I go inside and ask to speak with Nate Bishop under the pretense of purchasing pillows in bulk to distract Ricky, while Agent Haddon snatches the money from the car trunk?" Chief Lee knew his men were well trained and could pop open a trunk without a key in less than ten seconds. He felt confident that it could be done as long as Agent Marco kept Ricky occupied for at least three minutes.

"Yeah, go for it! Strike fast! Stay alert!" he warned.

The plan worked perfectly. Ricky explained to Agent Marco that one of his delivery guys was away in the Poconos and would be back on Monday. Mr. Bishop had suffered a major stroke and was barely hanging on to life, but the company would be continuing on. He and Mrs. Bishop would be running the business. Blah, blah, blah, blah he spoke on as he wrote down the fictitious name and address on the delivery slip, pausing every now and then for another answer from Agent Marco to complete the order.

"Okay," Ricky concluded, "I have six cases scheduled to be delivered next Friday. How would you like to pay? Bill you or pay upon delivery?"

"Actually," Agent Marco said, "I would like to pay upon delivery."

"Okay, no problem," Ricky said, extending his hand to seal the deal with a handshake. Agent Marco shook his hand and assured him he would see himself out.

"Finish up your paperwork and thank you so much," he said, hoping Agent Haddon had enough time to recover the money. "Please give my best wishes to Nate Bishop," he added.

Agent Haddon had worked quickly and efficiently. The three and a half million dollars was now in their unmarked police car. "We got the money!" Agent Haddon radioed to the chief. The chief was ecstatic to hear the news. "Stay alert guys! Good job!" commended the chief.

CHAPTER 33

Former Police Chief Dan Waters had a hard time sleeping and spent most of the night praying for Nate Bishop. He could not stop thinking of Nate and what might have really happened to him. He seemed fine that afternoon when they had lunch together. He arose early and decided to go to the hospital to check on him.

Just as he arrived at the hospital, Teresa and Ms. King arrived also. They rode in the elevator to the VIP suite together, but had never before met each other. They were all standing outside the door, waiting to enter Nate Bishop's room at the same time. Mrs. Bishop opened the door and was surprised to see them. She looked worn and exhausted, but tried hard not to let her trepidation and sadness show.

"Oh, so nice to see you all. I did not know you were all coming together to see Nate. He will be happy to see you all."

"Oh, Mrs. Bishop, this is Ms. Joni King, who is like a mother to me and Jamie. She is one with great faith! She wanted to come to pray for Nate." began Teresa.

"Oh sure, prayer is always good. Thank you Teresa and thank you Ms. King for coming," she said.

Ms. King smiled and gave her a comforting hug. Dan Waters extended his hand, and introduced himself to Ms. King and Teresa.

"I am Dan Waters, an old friend of Nate's. So nice to meet you both. If you all don't mind, I would like to stay and pray for Nate too."

"Well that will be great," as she motioned them into the room where Nate was resting. Many beautiful and colorful flowers and cards lined the windowsill expressing good wishes and a speedy recovery to Nate. They seemed to add life and hope to the room. Ms. King, Teresa, Dan and Mrs. Bishop walked over to the bed. Nate's eyes moved from one face to the next face. He actually focused on each person who stood before him. Mrs. Bishop smiled and rubbed his hair and said, "He knows you all are here. He can hear you and can communicate with you by blinking his eyes."

Teresa said, "Nate, it is so nice to see you. I brought my friend, Ms. King to pray with you." Nate blinked his eyes. Ms. King smiled and placed her hand on his shoulder.

"Is it okay if I pray for you now?" she asked.

Nate blinked again.

Mrs. Bishop and former Police Chief Waters stood on one side of his bed holding hands while Mrs. Bishop's free hand was placed on Nate's left hand. Ms. King and Teresa stood on the opposite side of the bed holding hands while Ms. King's free hand was placed on Nate's right hand. Chief Waters and Teresa reached across the bed to hold hands to make the circle complete around Nate. Ms. King began to sense the presence of God and His perfect Peace. There was a sweet stillness as the Glory of God connected to each person in the circle. In a small voice Ms. King heard these words again.

"I have need of you today my daughter. Yield yourself completely to Me I will use you for My Glory. I have sent you to lay hands on the sick today and Nate will recover. I am the God that heals. Jehovah Rophe is My Name!"

Tears flowed down Ms. Kings' face as she began to exalt God and surrender completely to Him. *"My heart, my mind, my soul belong to you Father. Use me for Your Glory Lord,"* she thought to herself as she began to pray out loud.

"Oh Father God, in Jesus Name, we thank You for Your presence and how wonderful You are to come here in this very room to see about Nate and each of us in this circle. We are humbled by Your presence. Father, I know You are moved with compassion as You look at Nate and his condition, and Father, I know there is nothing too hard for You, so I plead the Precious Blood of Jesus over Nate and ask for the manifestation of Your healing power to rest upon him and completely restore him." Ms. King's voice began to escalate as she said, *"I decree and declare the healing hand of God is upon you Nate Bishop and you shall rise once again to your rightful place in Christ Jesus. Paralysis must leave this body NOW! In the authority of Jesus Christ's Name I speak. You are healed, mind, body and soul NOW! In the Name above all Names, Jesus Christ, the Son of the Living God!"*

Nate's body began to shake violently and his breathing increased. He made stuttering sounds for the first time and gripped Mrs. Bishop's hand tightly. His face turned beet red and he then suddenly sat up straight in the bed! Mrs. Bishop's knees buckled and she fell to the floor, weeping loudly and praising God. Nate began to speak clearly, "Thank you Jesus! Thank you Jesus!" Everyone's mouth fell open in awe and wonder. There was not a dry eye in the room. All were standing in utter amazement as Nate swung his legs off the bed and stood up...completely healed! Overwhelmed with joy and the presence of God, he fell to the floor with his wife. No one seemed to notice that Nate's butt was exposed as the back of his hospital gown opened. They were oblivious to everything except the presence of God. They hugged, cried and praised God together on the floor. Those in the room witnessed a miracle and it would change their lives forever.

While this was transpiring, former Chief Waters was dancing and leaping and speaking in an unknown tongue. He had just experienced the Baptism into the Holy Spirit with the evidence of speaking in a language he did not know, nor did he understand what happened to him. He knew it was wonderful and whatever just occurred he never wanted it to end. There was a joy and peace as he had never known or could imagine. Teresa was elated and felt as if she could fly as she leaped and praised God in her unknown tongue.

Ms. King lay prostrate on the cold hospital floor praising God with Nate and Mrs. Bishop. After almost one hour of pure jubilee, Nate hugged and thanked Ms. King for the prayer and his healing, to which she quickly added, "I could not heal anyone. I was a willing vessel that Jesus wanted to use, but He and He alone healed you. He gets all the praise and glory!" Nate gave her yet another hug and crawled back into his bed. He said, "First I thank God I am healed but it is very important that this miracle is not shared with anyone outside this room. Teresa, I know you are not aware of what is going on, but Ricky has been smuggling drugs through my warehouse and threatened my life yesterday with a gun. He is using you Teresa to make labels to differentiate his boxes of drugs from my boxes of pillows. He is coming back here to kill me so he can take over Paradise Pillows. While I was paralyzed he came here and taunted me and told me how he was going to persuade you, Lola (looking at his wife), to let him continue to run the business." Teresa and Ms. Bishop stood with their eyes bulging out of their heads and mouths opened with disbelief. Teresa began to cry. Ms. Bishop grabbed the chair near his bed to steady herself because her legs buckled again. She felt sick and angry. She too was deceived and sweet-talked by Ricky.

"He seemed so worried about you Nate. How could I have been so trusting and foolish?" she stammered.

"It is okay Lola. He fooled a lot of us. We all trusted him."

"Oh my, Nate!" Teresa cried, "Ricky said he is coming to see you this afternoon. He is waiting for me to get back to the office. He was planning to go to the bank and then come see you. Oh God, what are we going to do?"

Ms. King moved in to comfort Teresa and assured everyone that everything was going to be fine. "God has ways of exposing the enemy and keeping His people safe. It is going to be okay," she spoke with authority, power and great confidence.

Former Police Chief Waters stepped closer and said, "Yes, you are right Ms. King. And don't you worry Teresa and Mrs. Bishop. I will call Police Chief Lee to handle this. He will know exactly what to do and how to do it so no one gets hurt. But please do as Nate said and do not breathe a word of this to anyone. Nate's life is at stake here. It is very important that everyone act as normal as possible when dealing with Ricky."

Teresa suddenly remembered Ricky had a key to her apartment and she had a key to his apartment. Her mind started racing. "Is he that dangerous that he will hurt me or Jamie?" she questioned. This was not the man she always knew. "We are his family. He loves us." She debated within herself, "But why does he have a gun? Why did he lie about Nate? I have to change the locks to my apartment. I must make sure Jamie and I are safe. What will I say to Rick when he questions why his key no longer works to my apartment? Too much to decipher now," she thought. "I will have a little more time to think later since I will not see him tonight because we are going to church with Momma King. I will figure out something," she thought.

CHAPTER 34

It was just before noon when Teresa returned to work. Paradise Pillows seemed to have a gloominess that Teresa had never noticed before. Was it because she knew Ricky was there waiting for her? She tried to convince herself over the rapid heartbeats that she was not afraid of him as she entered the building. It felt eerie, as if shadows were lurking in the hallway and behind each door, even though it was a bright sun shiny day outside. As she passed Nate's office, the image of Ricky holding the gun to Nate's head gave her cold chills and a queasy stomach. She hurried down the hall to her workstation speaking to a few of the other seamstresses along the way. Everyone was eager to know the status of Nate's condition.

"No change," she lied.

She was glad that Ricky was not in the office to greet her. She figured he was probably in his office or in the warehouse. Either way, she was grateful to have a moment to ponder all the things that she witnessed first-hand earlier. "I witnessed a miracle! Nate is completely healed and everyone in the room was filled with the Holy Spirit and spoke with unknown tongues." She began to weep at her workstation. She could feel the presence of

God as she began to praise His name softly so as to not bring attention to herself. She felt suddenly peaceful and relaxed. She did not notice Ricky as he approached until he was standing right in front of her.

"What's wrong Teresa?" he asked ever so gently.

Teresa jumped! She immediately felt angry and agitated that he interrupted her. She flashed her eyes and said "Nothing, I was feeling sorry for Nate," she lied. Ricky rushed around her workstation to comfort her. She promptly pushed him away. "No please don't," she resisted. Puzzled by her reaction he stepped back. "Did something happen to Nate? Is he dead?" he asked. "No, he is not dead!" she said abruptly, hoping to not create a scene at work. She said, "Could you please leave me alone! I need time to myself!"

"Wow!" he said, surprised by her harshness. "Well sure Babe. I am going to go to the bank and I will see you later. Hope you are feeling better," as he backed away from her workstation. Teresa nodded her head as she wiped the tears from her eyes which she could no longer suppress.

Teresa thought that while Ricky was gone she would call a locksmith to change the locks to her apartment. She left immediately from work to meet the locksmith. She was successful in getting the locks changed to her apartment all within an hour. She decided she would give the spare key to Momma King and go to her house and wait until it was time to go to church. "I definitely need a break from Ricky," she thought.

Ricky muttered to himself. "She has been acting really strange lately and very distant. Is she really that concerned about Nate or is it something more? Well, I can't worry about that right now. I got to get to the bank." He felt like a child on Christmas morning who just found everything he asked for underneath the tree. He was smiling and singing as he took the short walk to his car singing, 'I Feel Good' one of James Brown's classics. Just as he approached his car, he spun around and yelled, "Yeeeaaahhhh!!!" grinning from ear to ear as he made a pitiful attempt to mimic James Brown's Mashed Potatoes slide and stumbled into the car.

Agent Haddon and Agent Marcos laughed hysterically as they waited to see what he would do next. Haddon quieted himself in order to radio the chief.

"Subject is getting into his car" he reported.

Chief responded, "Follow him. The money has been secured, right?"

"Yes, money is in our possession," Haddon responded still suppressing his laughter.

"Follow him and give me his destination immediately." Chief directed.

"Roger that." Agent Haddon replied and hung the radio back in the holder. Agent Haddon and Agent Marco waited until Ricky left the parking lot and headed for the main road before they pulled out to follow him. Not sure where he was heading and not wanting to blow their cover, they followed with great caution, still laughing at Ricky's attempt to do the James Brown dance move.

CHAPTER 35

"Mr. Perez, it's me, Chico. I just arrived at Newark Airport and I'm on my way to get the U-Haul rental. I should be in place for the next pick-up in about an hour. Big Mc should be waiting when I get there."

Carlos Perez gave a sigh of relief. "Good, Chico. I hate having to send you there, but I need to make sure the job gets done and gets done right. There will be a nice bonus for you when you return. Be sure you let Big Mc know he will be minus a few thousand because of the breakdown in the operation. If he has any problems at all, eliminate him altogether. I can't have weak links!! Check in when pick-up is secured."

"Yes, Mr. Perez, I will be in touch."

Chico was not happy that he had to fly from Mexico to New Jersey because of Big Mc's mess up. "He better be there on time. The shipment better be in place and there better be nothing wrong or out of place or he is a dead man! Just the fact that I had to come all the way here is enough reason to kill him," he muttered angrily to himself after hanging up the phone.

****

The heavy smog was lifting as Big Mc exited Route 95 onto the narrow two lane highway. He was extremely grateful he was actually able to make it to Hoboken. Still in pain, he turned off the main road onto an unpaved single dirt road with grass patches in the middle of the path indicative of a sparsely traveled road. About a quarter of a mile in, the dirt road disappeared into an open parking lot. Finally, a row of warehouses sat in front of a large river with several boats docked in the water. It appeared to be a private marina owned by certain individuals who did not want to be known, indicated by the isolation and seclusion of the area. There was very little activity, only a few cars in the parking lot, and two gasoline pumps. Looking beyond the warehouses and river was an expanse of green meadows, filled with blooming wild flowers splashed haphazardly up the far distant mountain in myriad shades of yellow, orange, purple and red. It looked like a picture that only God could paint. It was all so stunning that Big Mc paused a moment to take it all in. In the midst of his pain, he smiled, in awe of God's creation and its beauty. He pulled the van into the parking lot and waited for the Pick-up. It was a little before 10 AM.

The two detectives deliberately passed the road which Big Mc turned onto to ensure they did not blow their cover. They drove about 200 feet down the main road and waited five minutes before turning back. Uncertain as to where the path would take them, they decided to take the gamble and if stopped they would pretend to be lost and trying to get back onto the interstate. Just as they drove into the clear, open parking lot, they immediately spotted Big Mc parked and appearing to be waiting for someone. They pretended to not notice Big Mc and drove directly toward the gas pumps and around to the back of the last warehouse. Big Mc watched them drive past him as if he was not there at all. "Oh, well, they are not here to see me," he said nonchalantly, as he continued to wait for Chico.

Out of sight and hoping no one noticed them, the two detectives quickly accessed the area, took many pictures of the boats as well as several visible cars along with their license plates. It appeared to be a road that circled around the warehouses and led back to the parking lot. Driving slowly, they found a perfect spot to observe Big Mc and anyone else approaching the building or the parking lot. Just as they were situated, a large U-Haul truck came into view in the parking lot. Big Mc recognized

Chico right away and gave him a quick head nod. Chico ignored him. He drove behind the van and parked the back of the U-Haul near the rear-end of the van, to make it easy to load the boxes into the U-Haul. Big Mc carefully got out of the van trying not to further injure himself.

Chico was very irritated and slammed the door as he got out of the truck. "It is because of you I had to fly here. Please just get out of my way," pushing Big Mc backwards. Big Mc winced in pain as he grabbed his stomach. Chico completely ignored his implication of pain. "And by the way, Mr. Perez gave me permission to eliminate you because of your screw up. Also you will be minus a few thousand from this shipment. If you have a problem with that call him!!"

Big Mc was completely caught off guard and remembered his gun was inside the van. He wondered how this was going to end. Could he get to his gun in case he needed it? Within five minutes all the boxes were loaded into the U-Haul. Chico wasted no time leaving with the shipment. His next drop-off was in Virginia. He had a six to eight hour drive and was not in the mood for friendly chit chat. He resented having to be there. Big Mc sighed with relief as Chico drove off.

The two detectives took pictures of Chico removing the boxes of drugs marked *BOYS* from the van and putting them in his U-Haul. They radioed in and informed the chief of what just had transpired as they headed out, passing Big Mc. Then suddenly the chief gave word to go back and arrest Big Mc, making sure he can't inform anyone of the bust that was going down. Chief advised, "We have an unmarked car in place at the next exit that will tail the U-Haul to its destination. Bring Big Mc back here." Just as Chief planned, when the drugs were transported and en route to the next stop, the driver delivering would be arrested and detained for at least 24 hours without a phone call. It would work like a domino effect. Chico was arrested shortly after the drop in Virginia and the Feds followed the new driver and his companion to the next drop in Florida where they too were both arrested trying to smuggle the boxes onto a small private airplane. It was believed the plane belonged to Mr. Perez, but it could not be proven. The plane was also confiscated with all the boxes of drugs and held by the federal undercover narcotic agents who made the arrest. It was a smooth and tight operation and Chief 'Hawkeye' Lee was extremely pleased. After several years of investigative and undercover work, the East Coast drug trafficking was finally being annihilated. "Outstanding police work!" he beamed.

Mr. Perez cussed and slammed the phone down when he was not able to make contact with Chico and Big Mc. It had been over fifteen hours and he could not make contact with anyone. He knew something was wrong. "This is all Big Mc's fault," he yelled out of frustration. "He is a dead man!"

CHAPTER 36

Margie was so excited as she left her apartment to go to the church meeting that evening she walked out without her keys or pocketbook. But she had the most important thing... her old Bible given to her by her grandmother when she turned thirteen. She was actually nervous as if she were going on her first date with the man of her dreams. Indirectly, she was. Meeting Jesus was the best and most perfect date ever!!

The one thousand seat edifice was full of people smiling and hugging each other as they all began to take their seats. Margie hung back briefly scanning the audience for Shironi. "It feels so good to be in church," she thought. The smell of the old pine pews brought back many memories of when her grandmother would take her to church. It seemed like she was a little girl again at home with Grandma. It all seemed so familiar. Everyone smiled and greeted her with care and love. She was filled with such joy that she was overwhelmed and tears began to flow down her cheeks. The usher moved quickly to give her a genuine hug and tissues to dry her eyes.

"Welcome to Light of Love Ministries," she said, motioning her to a seat nearby. Shironi tapped the usher lightly on the shoulder and said, "She is with me." Smiling, the usher gave Shironi a hug and escorted them to a seat far to the front of the church.

Margie grabbed Shironi's hand, "I can't stop crying," she said. "I feel so good inside and yet I am crying."

Shironi just smiled and told her, "That always happens when you are in the presence of pure love. God is Love and His Spirit is here. Just enjoy and feel free to express yourself as you like."

Teresa, Jamie and Ms. King made their way up to the front and took the pew just behind Shironi and Margie. Shironi turned to greet Mother King as she was known in church. Mother King was a strong woman of faith. Many of the younger women always seemed to gravitate to her. She was loved and adored by everyone, including Pastor Sherman and his wife, Lady Joyce. Shironi quickly introduced everyone to each other. They all hugged each other and settled back in their pews.

An instant hush seemed to have fallen and suddenly the praise team was singing and everyone joined in. Some had their eyes closed as they sang, while others raised their hands in complete acquiescence to the Spirit of God, yet others sobbed quietly in their pews, including Margie and Teresa.

Teresa was ecstatic and could hardly contain herself. She suddenly realized how awesome God really was. He healed Nate, filled everyone in the hospital room this morning with His Holy Spirit and now she is actually experiencing another height of ecstasy. Without any effort on her part, she began to praise God in a language she did not know she could speak, yet she knew exactly what she was saying but it was not in English. Teresa made a mental note to be sure to ask Momma King what was happening to her. She loved it. It felt incredibly beautiful.

Jamie's eyes were huge and bulging with excitement as he tried to sing the unfamiliar songs and mimic others worshipping God. He loved the church experience and was feeling the presence of God as well. Soon the worship was over and the first speaker, Minister Martinez came to the pulpit. She was a young woman who looked to be in her early twenties yet spoke with such power and maturity that it almost seemed unnatural. There was definitely something peculiar about her as she spoke with such conviction and authority. She appeared to know everything about Margie. Margie sat on the edge of the pew and hung onto each word. Minister Martinez shared her life story about being raped at the age of nine by one of her mother's boyfriends. She had a great relationship with her father, although they did not live in the same house. She loved and adored her father.

She shared that the biggest pain and guilt she experienced was when she told her father about the man who raped her. Her father waited outside her mother's house until the man arrived and then killed him. He was now incarcerated in a prison down south sixteen hours away. She was only able to see him once or twice a year. She missed him so much. She had blamed herself that he was taken from her. "If she had only kept quiet he would still be with her," she thought over and over again. Feeling lonely and void of her father's love, she became very promiscuous. By the age of seventeen she had experienced three abortions and was hopelessly miserable. She began to visit fortune tellers in the hope of a brighter future. Eventually, she sold her body to get money to give to the fortune teller who made many false predictions and blamed her when things did not happen as predicted. The fortune teller made her feel ashamed and guilty, implying there were things in her life that were causing her to be cursed. The remedy was that she must bring more money to break the curses. Minister Martinez had become a slave trying to find freedom from her past only to discover she was going deeper into the occult and witchcraft. She and the fortune teller had performed many rituals and chanted many spells but to no avail.

"One day," Minister Martinez said, as she turned and pointed to Mother King, "*this* woman of God saw me in the supermarket and told me that Jesus loved me and that He had a special plan for my life. She invited me here to this church two years ago and my life changed. I now understand the purpose and plan God has for my life. Not in its totality, but enough to know He loves me and called me to preach His Glorious Gospel."

Margie could not control her tears. It was as if God were speaking directly to her and about her own involvement with the psychic, Madame Zoe. Minister Martinez called her to the altar and laid hands upon her and spoke peace to her mind and soul. Margie felt overwhelmed with a love she had never known before. She remained at the altar the rest of the service, weeping.

Several other young preachers took the podium and boldly declared the power of God with signs and wonders that followed. The last to minister was Brother Stevenson who prophesied. *"There is a young lady here who is being deceived, and you are in danger, but God will deliver you because He has a big plan for your life. He is going to use you in a mighty way, and remember no matter how painful your experience may be, there is good going to come from it. God's hand is upon you and you belong to Him. Please come now so I can pray for you."* Teresa felt a tug on her heart as if God was again talking only to her. She did not go up for prayer because she would then have to explain some things to Momma King, so she thought. Teresa sat still and continued to pray, while tears streamed down her face. *"God please be with me and Jamie and help us,"* she cried within.

Pastor Sherman took the pulpit and made the final remarks. He was so proud of each of the young preachers and thanked them so much for their honesty and candidness. He invited each visitor to come back on Sunday, encouraged everyone to love each other and then gave the benediction. Everyone began to stir and greet each other. Some were still crying and hugging each other.

Margie was still at the altar weeping when Ms. King, Teresa and Jamie left. Shironi sat quietly praying as she witnessed God's amazing love saturate Margie. Margie was indeed a new creature in Christ!

CHAPTER 37

Ricky drove to Compton Trust and Loan Bank. He sat in the car a few minutes and decided to first go in and obtain the safety deposit box before bringing in his millions. Ricky entered the bank feeling just like the millions he believed was in his trunk. He smiled at several of the tellers before making his way to Mr. Wenzel, the bank manager. Ricky had a great rapport with Mr. Wenzel. They talked like old friends when Ricky set up the bank account in Jamie and Teresa's name. Mr. Wenzel was very impressed with the love he portrayed for Jamie, his future stepson and Teresa, his finance. He thought it was such a noble thing to do for the woman he loved and her son. Just as Ricky approached the door, Mr. Wenzel looked up over his glasses and motioned for Ricky to come into his office, as he finished his phone call.

"Ahhh, Mr. Clay," as he reached out extending his hand, "It is so nice to see you. Are you ready to set up the safe deposit box you mentioned before?" Smiling and returning the handshake Ricky replied, "Yes, today is the day." They quickly sat down to complete the business. Within ten minutes the transaction was complete and Ricky was given the key to the safe deposit box. Ricky stood smiling and thanked Mr. Wenzel, promising to be back in a few minutes.

Ricky walked out to the street heading for his car. He was breathing heavily from the exhilaration of having three and a half million dollars laying in his trunk. His beeper started to buzz. It was Dante and Billy confirming their arrival time to celebrate their millions. They would be meeting with Ricky at his apartment later that evening. He was euphoric. His ego, arrogance and smugness made him feel like he was a part of Elliott Ness's team, "The Untouchables." He opened the trunk of his car. There were no duffel bags and no money! Paralyzed with fear, Ricky felt his breath leave his body and his legs collapsed as he fell to the ground. Sweating and crying, he inhaled deeply to get some air into his lungs. "Is this a dream? This could not be happening!" he thought. He pulled himself up and peered into the trunk again, thrashing his arms haphazardly around the trunk, cursing and hissing like a caged animal who was searching for his last meal, which was obviously not there. Frustrated and in a rage, he kicked the rear end of the car smashing his shin against the bumper causing more profanity and excruciating pain. Ricky looked up and down the street trying to see anyone who looked suspicious and who could have possibly taken his money. Visibly, there was no one in sight to blame.

Ricky slowly closed the trunk and limped back into the car. He sat quietly trying to put the pieces together, retracing everything in his mind over and over again. Who could have possibly known the money was in the trunk of his car? "Big Mc and possibly Teresa," as he recalled seeing her in the parking lot of Paradise shortly after Big Mc left. "There is no way he could have doubled back and stolen the money, and still have made the delivery to New Jersey on time." Big Mc had beeped him when Chico arrived to inform him that the connection was complete. Ricky was surprised Chico had flown in from Mexico to make this delivery. He knew that if Chico was the one to carry out the delivery Mr. Perez must be infuriated and it could mean Big Mc's life. But this did not faze Ricky, nor did he care as long as he and the *BOYS* had their cut. Cursing and feeling nauseated, Ricky vowed that whoever had double-crossed him would pay dearly. "No one disrespects me in this way," he muttered. "No one," thinking of Teresa and the way she had acted earlier at the office. "She did not want me to touch her and what was she crying about? It couldn't have just been about Nate Bishop," he thought, "but I am going back to the office to get some answers." Trying to calm himself down, he started to take deep breaths and exhaled slowly. He was hyperventilating and nothing could bring him back to normal. "What will the *BOYS* think? What will I tell them?" he thought as he headed back to Paradise Pillows.

Agent Haddon and Marcos could hardly contain themselves as they watched Ricky's extravaganza unfold. They almost felt sorry for him *after* they stopped laughing. They went into the bank to ask questions. They identified themselves and spoke with Mr. Wenzel. He was very helpful and informed them that Ricky was an amazing man. He had opened up a business account for his fiancée and another account for his fiancée's son, Mr. Wenzel recalled. "I remember his name. It is Jamie. He is not the biological father. He wants it to be a surprise for Jamie when he turns eighteen. He put his pastor's name, Rev. Dante who lives in Florida on it to oversee the money. He also opened up a business account for his girl so when she retires she would have a nice little nest egg saved up for her. He just came in today and opened up a safe deposit box. He said he would be right back, but he has not returned yet. Is he okay?"

"Oh, yes, he is okay, we are just doing some routine work," Agent Haddon said. They both thanked Mr. Wenzel and left their business card with him suggesting he call them if he remembered anything more.

Ricky quickly noticed Teresa's car was no longer in the parking lot. He needed answers. He slammed the door behind him as he entered the office. Teresa's assistant, Leslie, greeted him smiling in spite of the obvious look of upset on his face. "Oh, what is wrong?" she asked, not sure how to act. Ricky was never angry. He was always happy and very respectable and drop dead gorgeous! He inquired of Teresa's whereabouts. She told him that Teresa had left for the day and did not say where she was going.

"Actually", she smiled again mischievously. "I thought you both were having an afternoon rendezvous. You know, when the cat is away the mice will play," she said jokingly. Ricky did not laugh or even acknowledge her innuendo. Leslie was embarrassed and tried to redeem herself by getting back to business.

"Oh by the way," she said, "Sal came back today from the Poconos. He said to let you know he would be in tomorrow morning, but if you need him this afternoon to give him a call at home, his phone service has been restored."

"I will not be back this afternoon," he grunted, slamming the door as he left.

"Wow!" Leslie thought. "He and Teresa must have had a little fight. They always seemed to be so in love. Well, I guess no matter how much in love you are, every once in a while a fight is inevitable." Leslie smiled at the idea of being in love and having a fight, knowing in her heart, that it would only last a minute. She had been lonely for a long time and she would not entertain any fighting. She laughed out loud and went back to her workstation thinking how lucky Teresa was to have a man like Ricky Clay.

Ricky arrived at Teresa's house, did not see her car, and was deeply disturbed that she was not home. "Where could she be? At the bank depositing my money?" he thought sarcastically. He sat in his car not knowing where to go or what to do. "The contact was made in New Jersey and Big Mc had made the delivery, so there is no way he could have doubled back without being seen," he reasoned. "It had to be Teresa," he decided, as he reflected on her mannerism earlier that afternoon at work.

"The *BOYS* will be here later this evening and I have no money for them or myself. What should I tell them, that my girl double-crossed me? How humiliating *that* will be? Will they believe me or think I am lying?" Ricky felt sick to his stomach as he slumped over the steering wheel. "Where could Teresa possibly be?" he wondered. He waited several hours and then remembered she was going to church with Ms. King. With no place else to go, except home, and not wanting to deal with Billy and Dante without having the money, he decided to go inside her apartment to wait and confront her when she came home. He had to know where she hid the money before facing the *BOYS*. He figured they would be at his apartment by now. Trying each key on his key ring left him furious that none of the keys allowed him to access Teresa's apartment. "When did she change the locks on her doors? I will kill her!" he cursed, convinced all the more that she had somehow stolen the money from the trunk and now had locked him out.

Dante and Billy could hardly contain their excitement at seeing Ricky again and of course the big celebration of their *score of a lifetime.* Billy and Dante met at JFK Airport and rented a car. They drove the hour ride to Ricky's house chatting about what they were going to do with their split of the money. Dante and Billy had decided that they were going to get out of the business. Reflecting on the many things the *Boy*s had been through together in life, gave them the confidence that they could persuade Ricky into getting out as well. They were *covenant brothers* and their day had finally arrived and things were going to be different for the rest of their lives. A dream had come true for the *BOYS*.

CHAPTER 38

Teresa and Jamie were so excited and full of joy as they returned to Ms. King's house to get their car. Teresa had many questions about her experience in church, but decided she would talk about it with Ms. King tomorrow because it was getting late. They quickly hugged each other and said their good-byes as Jamie opened the car door for his mother.

Ms. King smiled, "Wow Jamie, you have become such a gentleman." Jamie beamed from ear to ear shaking his head in agreement.

"Yes, M'am, Ricky told me I should always open the door for my momma." Teresa smiled and graciously sat down, having a proud momma moment. She started the car and waited until Jamie buckled himself into his seat belt. "Momma King, I got a lot of things I want to talk to you about. I will stop by tomorrow evening okay?" she yelled, as she drove off.

No one noticed the dark shadow that was lurking near the entrance to their apartment as Teresa fumbled for her new key. Suddenly she felt fearful remembering she had changed the lock and had only given Ms. King the extra key to her apartment. "I will think of something to tell Ricky tomorrow as to why I changed the locks," she thought as a cold chill ran through her body. Just as she opened the door, Jamie went in first flipping the light switch on as he entered. Teresa followed behind. When she turned to close the door, Ricky appeared from out of nowhere. Jamie, excited as usual to see Ricky, ran to him. Teresa tried to smile but fear and fright was plastered on her face. Ricky patted Jamie on the head and told him, "Your mom and I got some business to discuss. Go get ready for bed okay?" They did their little special handshake and Jamie left the room. Teresa was shivering with fear. Trying not to feel intimidated and fearful, she walked over to the couch and sat down. Ricky following directly behind her.

"So you changed the locks and stole my money, huh?" Ricky accused.

"What are you talking about?" she frowned.

"My money, Teresa, where is it?" You are the only one who could have taken it. I know you have it someplace and I don't want to hurt you. So please, please Teresa, tell me where my money is...NOW!!" Teresa jumped as his voice snapped loudly. She continued to protest that she did not have a clue as to what he was talking about. Without another word spoken, Ricky's temper flared and Teresa felt a sharp blow to the side of her head. Knocked unconscious with one punch, Ricky tied her hands and carried her to his car and strapped her in with the seatbelt. He quickly raced back to get Jamie and plundered the small apartment. He searched everywhere but to no avail. There were no duffel bags or money anywhere. Ricky decided to leave, thinking maybe she had it stashed somewhere at the office or maybe Ms. King's house. Still unaware of the dangers and trusting Ricky, Jamie did as he was told and climbed into the back seat of the car. Jamie thought his mother was sleeping as they pulled out of the parking lot heading towards their favorite fishing hole on the outskirts of town.

CHAPTER 39

Chief Lee moved quickly to get to the hospital after speaking with former Chief Dan Waters. He ordered Agent Haddon to arrest Ricky Clay and book him for drug trafficking and with specific orders... "No phone calls to anyone for 48 hours." Chief Lee wanted to be sure Ricky could do no further harm to Nate Bishop as well as not be able to notify anyone of his arrest until Chief Lee could get as many of his thugs off the streets and in jail as possible.

Arriving at the hospital, Chief 'Hawkeye' Lee and one of his undercover agents, briefed Nate Bishop and Lola of their plan to register them into a private five star hotel for a few days to keep them safe until Ricky was behind bars. The nurses and doctors were briefed as well. They were to advise anyone coming to visit Nate that he had been moved to a private room as per doctor's orders and no visitors were allowed. Nate and Lola were still rejoicing at the complete recovery and the miracle God had performed when Dr. Hughes entered the room. He was completely astonished and said that in all of his twenty years of practicing, he had never seen a recovery of this magnitude. "This is a miracle!" he exclaimed in disbelief. He checked all of Nate's vitals, shook his hand, and gave

Lola a warm hug. They thanked the doctor as Nate quickly put on his disguise of a long trench coat, top hat and thick black mustache that Chief Lee gave him to wear. He also brought a blonde wig for Lola. Lola laughed at their new look as she exited the room to get the rented car waiting for her. Chief Lee advised Lola to leave her personal car in the parking lot just in case someone was watching the car. She quickly got into the waiting car and drove to the designated hotel and checked in under the alias name of 'Sallie Griffin'. Chief Lee arrived within minutes with Nate. Lola was still in the lobby and quickly joined her husband as Chief Lee escorted them to their private suite. "Please don't leave the suite for any reason," was his final instruction after spending about fifteen minutes gathering information about Ricky, Teresa, Sal and everyone associated with the warehouse at Paradise Pillows.

"Here's my direct number. Call me if you need anything or something new comes to mind. I want you here and safe until I find Ricky Clay and put him where he belongs. I will contact you tomorrow and let you know when I have him in custody. Everything is here. No need to go out. There is plenty of fresh fruit, vegetables, eggs, cold cuts, steaks and lamb chops in the fridge including pastries as well as drinks of all kinds. Here's an electric stove if you chose to cook, pointing toward the stove. But if you need anything, anything at all, just let me know."

Nate assured Chief that it was sufficient and everything would be fine. Lola felt alive and beautiful both inside and out. She was still trying to wrap her mind around the miracle she witnessed earlier that morning. So full of joy, she just wanted to snuggle up with Nate in front of the fireplace in the sunken living room with popcorn, wine and cheese. Nate was in total agreement. They enjoyed the quietness and each other as they watched movies, sipped wine and snuggled. Lola wanted it to be a special night for Nate. They both felt as if it was their honeymoon and decided to take advantage of this wonderful opportunity to embrace each other and the moment. Lola wanted to ask questions, but decided she would wait until tomorrow. She would be the *newly-wed bride* tonight as Nate took her hand and lead her up to the oversized bedroom with a huge hot tub lined with candles. Smokey Robinson was singing softly on the radio, "Turn the lights down low and baby come close..." Lola thought, "Oh how appropriate that song was," as she quickly lit all of the candles, adding a special romantic radiance to the room.

"Awwh, this is perfect," Nate said softly, as he and Lola disrobed and entered into the hot tub. They were completely lost in each other and so grateful for another opportunity to live life to its fullest, in good health and with each other.

CHAPTER 40

Billy and Dante made themselves comfortable in Ricky's apartment as they waited for him to return. The fridge was full of snacks, cold cuts, champagne and beer. It looked like Ricky had prepared a celebration for them. They had spoken to Ricky earlier and he told them that he would be arriving shortly after they got in. He was going to settle a few things and would join them later. It was now past midnight and no Ricky, and no phone call...no contact at all. It was as if he had disappeared. Billy and Dante looked at each other. Neither could not bring themselves to say what they both were thinking. Did Ricky double-cross them? They showered and decided they would ride around town to see if they could find Big Mc or Ricky. They went to the club where they had all met years earlier. It was pretty quiet. No one had seen Big Mc at all that evening. They hung out there and had a few drinks. It was not the same without Ricky. They avoided eye contact with each other, yet knowing in their gut something was terribly wrong. They stayed until the club closed at 3 AM and then headed back to Ricky's apartment. Billy and Dante both could not hold back their disappointment when Ricky's car was still not visible and he obviously was not at home.

Neither wanted to admit that it was possible Ricky had double-crossed them and took all the money for himself.

Dante remembered that Ricky had showed him where Teresa lived when he came to visit last year but had not gotten the chance to meet her.

"Hey Man, let's take a ride to his girl's house. It is not too far from here."

"Yeah, sure Man. Let's see if he is there. He got a lot of explaining to do, Man. I am starting to get deeply disturbed right now. I can't bring myself to even say what I am thinking. Just the thought of what I am thinking breaks my heart. I know this can't be true. Ricky loves us like we are blood, Man. No way would he double cross us like this."

Dante could only nod his head as they turned onto the street where Teresa lived. It was the only apartment that had lights on at that hour in the morning. They quickly parked their car and walked up to her apartment door. There was no need to knock because the door was slightly ajar. Dante and Billy quickly entered the apartment and closed the door behind them. The apartment was very neat and orderly with the exception of a few dresser drawers which were opened and some clothes hanging out in Teresa and Jamie's bedroom.

Billy said, "Man, it looks like they may have left here in a rush with clothes hanging out of the drawers and the door not even shut. Her pocketbook is here on the couch with $37.00 in it and her keys are right by the door. I wish I knew what kind of car she drove. I wonder if it is out there in the parking lot."

"Yeah Man, let's get out of here. We don't want the neighbors calling the police and saying they saw two men coming from her apartment around 3 or 4 AM.

"Yeah Man," Dante said, moving toward the door. "We have no other choice but to wait for Ricky at his place. If he doesn't show up tonight, we will find the location of the warehouse and pay it a visit tomorrow. We need some answers and we will find some tomorrow for sure!" Billy could sense Dante was getting more and more agitated. Dante was always easy going but when he felt betrayed or disrespected, he was known to become a dangerous, heartless, and cruel man. He showed no mercy to his victims.

Billy said, "I am sure there is a reason for all this. Let's not jump to a conclusion yet. Maybe something really bad happened to Rick. I checked all the local hospitals and no one by the name of Ricky Clay was admitted. Let's get some rest and go to his workplace in a few hours. It is 4 AM now," looking at his flashy gold watch. "I guess we can get a few hours sleep and go to Paradise Pillows around 8 or 9 AM to check on him. Who knows, maybe he is already back in his apartment by now wondering where we are." Dante waved his hand at Billy, in disbelief and total disgust as they both left the apartment.

"Yeah right," he muttered under his breath.

****

Ms. King was feeling very excited as she waved goodbye to Jamie and Teresa and hurried into her house. She reflected on the Power of God that healed Nate Bishop and filled him with the Baptism of the Holy Spirit, with the evidence of speaking in tongues. She could hardly contain the joy that bubbled up inside of her and began to praise God for everything that happened, including the powerful church service where many were healed and delivered from tormenting spirits. Just as she entered the door of her house, she was suddenly in a place that looked unfamiliar but yet familiar to her. It was the same old dingy dilapidated house that she saw a while back in a vision. There it was again, and she sensed somehow that Jamie and Teresa were there and in danger. Ms. King did not understand. She had just dropped them off and they both were so excited about their experiences at church. Nevertheless, Ms. King knew God wanted her to pray earnestly for them. She fell prostrate on the floor and began to plead the Blood of Jesus over them. *"Shield them O Lord from all harm and danger. Please keep them safe from the hand of the evil one. I plead Your Blood over them now, and we know nothing can penetrate Your Blood. Thank you Jesus, thank you God and thank you Holy Spirit for a divine intervention."*

Soon a peace passed over her again, just as it had before. She knew that whatever danger they may be in or will encounter, they would be fine. She got up and made a hot cup of tea and phoned Teresa. There was no answer. She remembered the message Pastor Sherman preached a while back...*Why Pray and Worry?* Ms. King did not worry. She believed and trusted God that He would protect them no matter what.

CHAPTER 41

The dirt road to the old abandoned shack was very bumpy and totally isolated. The full moon made the shack look very uninviting and creepy. The boards that framed the shack curved upward and buckled outward from the erosion of rain and snow over years of exposure to the harsh weather; making gaping cracks for all creatures to crawl or slither in. It was very eerie and scary all the more at this time of night. Ricky and the *BOYS* once used the shack as a hang-out to party, drink, and stash their drugs. Ricky passed the fishing hole that he and Jamie often fished in and headed on toward the one room shack. Although it was very dark, Jamie recognized the area and became more inquisitive.

"Are we going fishing tonight Rick?

" No, not tonight Little Man, I am trying to keep you and your momma safe from some real bad guys and I need you to be a big man. Now, I am going to put you and your mother in this old shack. I got your mother's hands tied up now. I will tie up her feet when I get you both in the shack, just to make sure she can't get away and go back to your house. I got to keep you and her safe. So when she wakes up, promise me you will not untie her hands and feet until I come back. I am going to take care of the bad guys that want to hurt you and your mother. Do you understand me Jamie?"

"Yes, Ricky but it is very dark in here and I am scared. Please don't leave us here. Can we go with you?" he pleaded on the verge of tears.

"Listen Jamie, I need you to be a *Man* now and take care of your mother. Can I trust you or should I tie you up too?"

" No," Jamie said, "I will stay here with momma and you don't have to tie me up," trying to sound like a big guy.

"I have to go now but I will be back soon. Do not untie your mother because she will go back to the house and you both can be killed. Please Jamie I need you to be a big man now, okay?"

"Okay Ricky," as they did their special hand shake.

"That's my Man," as he rubbed Jamie on the head.

Teresa appeared to be sleeping as he tied her to a wooden chair with broken slats. Ricky lit an old candle that reflected shadows and silhouettes on the walls of the shack, causing an even greater creepiness.

"I will be back soon!" he yelled, as he got back into his car and drove off.

Ricky's mind was going a mile a minute. "Did Teresa have anything to do with the disappearance of the money? If she didn't, then who? This may be the best place for her and Jamie now if I can't convince Dante and Billy that I did not double cross them. They will think I am lying and maybe try to harm Teresa and Jamie. Yes, this is best for now, until I can speak to the *BOYS* and figure out who has the money. What will I tell them?" Ricky tried to convince himself that they would listen to him and believe him, but he could not believe it himself. "Oh, well, I will see them in a few minutes," as he headed toward his apartment. "They have been waiting for me all night. They gotta believe me. They know me. We are *covenant brothers*. We are the *BOYS*," he thought.

Jamie sat on the old musty cushion too afraid to move. He waited for a long time watching his mother in the dimly lit room. Finally, Teresa woke up. She had a throbbing headache. "Oh God, help me! Where am I?" she cried. "I gotta get Jamie...huh?" as she tried to get up, suddenly aware of her inability to move and her surroundings. Jamie spoke up, trying to calm his mother.

"Momma, I am here with you. Ricky will be back soon to get us. He is going to get the bad guys that want to hurt us. He brought us here so we can be safe."

"What? What are you talking about Jamie? Where are we? Why are we here?" Her head was pounding. Confused and trying to make sense of her predicament, Teresa called to Jamie.

"Jamie, come here and untie my hands."

"No Mommy, I can't untie your hands until Ricky comes back."

"Jamie, it is okay, Remember I told you if you are ever lost or kidnapped and afraid what you should do?"

"Yes, but there are no phones and no policemen here to call for help."

"That's right, Jamie. That's why you must untie my hands and feet so I can go get help. The bad guys can come to get us here."

"No Momma, Ricky said he was going to get the bad guys and he will come back to get us. I have to protect you, Momma, because Ricky doesn't want you to go to the house because the bad guys are there waiting to get us."

"Jamie, listen to me. I will not go home. But I am really afraid to be here in this place, and I need your help to untie my hands. We will go to the police so we can be safe and I will call Ricky to let him know where we are, okay?"

Reluctantly, Jamie agreed. The plastic cord Ricky used to tie Teresa's hands was very tight and hard. Jamie tried and tried until it was almost daybreak outside. His little fingers were hurting. He managed to get it loose enough, so Teresa could finish it with her teeth. Finally her hands were free. Now, the task of loosening her feet and getting out of there before Ricky returns. "Where are we? Where could Jamie and I run to?" she thought.

Unbeknownst to Teresa, shortly after Ricky had left them in the shack and turned onto the main interstate back into the city, Agent Marco spotted his car going in the opposite direction. He quickly made a u-turn and called for backup and followed him. Ricky decided to go to Paradise Pillows before going to his apartment. He needed some answers. Agent Marco waited until Ricky parked his car. As soon as Ricky stepped out of the car, Agent Marco and his backup team rushed in and arrested him and confiscated his car as well. Ricky was speechless and surrendered without a fight.

"But why does this man (Agent Marco) look so familiar to me?" he kept thinking.

CHAPTER 42

Carolyn was still in the mood to be catered to so suggested she and Sal have a late Friday night snack at Lil Elite. They had such a wonderful time in the Poconos and she did not want it to end. Sal opened his soul to his wife. He shared with her his fears about being abused as a young boy. For the first time he confessed why he was afraid to have children. It was not because they could not afford them or that he did not want children. It was because of the abuse he suffered as a boy at the hands of his father. He was fearful of being a failure like his father. Now he was no longer afraid. He wanted to have children more than ever. Carolyn was ecstatic at the idea of being a mother and for the first time she understood Sal in a way she had never known. She empathized with him and realized how painful it was for him to share all that with her. He had always suppressed his hurt and his true feelings, but she knew him well enough to know that he really loved her and wanted his love reciprocated.

Sal understood now, that no matter what happens in his life he had to stay in fellowship with God and praise Him for everything. He knew in his heart that it was God who had been missing from his life all this time. He knew it was God who had restored his marriage. He knew it was God who had changed his heart and gave him the job. He knew it was God who healed his heart from his childhood pain. He didn't want to sound like a fanatic but Sal took advantage of every opportunity to share his faith with Carolyn and reassured her that things would only get better. Oftentimes, he could not suppress his tears. He reflected on the conversation he had with Ricky before going to the Poconos and how the Power of God touched Ricky causing him to weep. Carolyn listened not only with her ears, but with her heart. She too began to weep. She felt a deeper love and compassion for Sal as never before. He was still Sal, but so different somehow. Whatever the difference was, she loved it.

"Well, tomorrow I am going to stop by the warehouse to see if Ricky needs me." Sal looked surprised to see it was 10 PM when he looked at this watch.

"Wow, Babe, it's getting late. Let's go home," as he stood to help her up.

"Okay Sal," Carolyn said, looking up into his eyes. "I want you to know that I appreciate you and all that you have done for me. I have felt like the most beautiful woman in the world these last few days, and it is all because of you. I love you Sal Tully."

"I love you too Carolyn Tully," as he stooped down and kissed her softly on the lips.

****

In the meantime, Margie was finally able to get up from the altar about a half hour later after the church service was over. Shironi stayed with her, encouraging her to completely surrender everything to God. Margie felt so wonderful. It felt like she had cried a river of tears...tears that liberated her from the pain of her past. Just as Margie arrived at home, Sal and Carolyn arrived as well. Although it was still dark, Sal and Carolyn noticed there was something different about Margie. She seemed to have a peace and a radiance about her that they had never noticed before. Bubbling over with joy and happiness, Margie rushed over to them.

"Listen you guys. Something wonderful just happened to me. I gave my life to Jesus and He has forgiven me of all my sins. Please, I would like to invite you both to come to church on Sunday." Surprised by her excitement, Carolyn could not help but be happy for her just as Sal was. "Wow!" Carolyn said, "I have been told all weekend about how great Jesus is," smiling at Sal. "I guess it is destined for me to experience Jesus too. It seems I can't get around or away from it. Sal and I would love to come Margie."

Sal, could hardly believe his ears. Sal joined in, "Yes, I was trying to decide which church I wanted to go to myself. This is like another answer to prayer."

Margie and Carolyn took the lead as they walked to their apartments. Margie was telling her of the preaching and fellowship she had experienced at church earlier. Carolyn was genuinely excited for her and now more than ever, curious to have the same encounter. Sal followed behind and listened as Margie shared her experience and her transformation at the altar.

"She does not seem like the same seductive woman that almost cost me my marriage. Just look at the two of them talking like old friends. You would never have known that a few months ago, they actually had a fight in almost this same spot," as he looked down at the paved walkway. "Look at God! He really knows how to change the heart of a person," he marveled.

"If it wasn't so late, I would invite you in so you can tell us more about it," Carolyn said.

Margie agreed. "Yes, perhaps another time. Maybe we can get together Sunday after church for dinner. Sunday service is at 10AM at The Light of Love Church located on the corner of Prospect and Newfoundland Street." Margie said.

"Yes, that sounds great. We know where it is. We will be there." Carolyn promised and said, "Good night."

CHAPTER 43

The moon seemed to replicate shadows behind every tree. A creepy and eerie feeling flooded Teresa and she could hardly breathe. She shivered as fear gripped every cell in her body. She remembered the prophetic word that was given to warn her of being deceived and in danger. She knew without a doubt that Brother Stevenson was referring to her. "Maybe if I had obeyed and let him pray for me I would not be in this predicament now," she thought. She held tight to Jamie's hand as they began their walk. Unsure of her location and surroundings, she could only pray that she was going in the right direction. Teresa was grateful she had changed into her flat driving shoes when she left church with Ms. King earlier that evening. It would have been very difficult to walk in high heels on that rocky dirt road. The sound of crickets and owls hooting filled the late night air causing her to squeeze Jamie's hand tighter. Jamie broke the silence.

"Mama you are hurting my hand," he complained tugging, trying to free his hand. "Oh, Baby, I am sorry, I just want to make sure you hold on to me and..." Interrupting her, Jamie exclaimed, "Oh Mama, this is the place where Ricky takes me fishing," pulling his hand free pointing to the little pond that Teresa did not even notice.

"Really Baby? Do you know how to get out of here?"

"Yes, Mama, just keep walking this way and we will get out," pointing straight in front of them. Teresa felt relieved for a fleeting moment. Then she suddenly remembered. Fear had immobilized her to the point that she had forgotten she could pray. *"Oh Jesus, please help me and Jamie get to safety. Take away my fears now, Lord please. In Jesus Name."*

It was about 5:30 in the morning when they reached the interstate. Teresa held Jamie very close to her. It was very dangerous to be walking on a major interstate. Cars and trucks drove by at a high rate of speed causing heavy dust and debris to settle on their clothes and in their hair. They had been walking for about twenty minutes when a police car drove up behind them. Looking very disheveled and relieved, Teresa began to sob uncontrollably. "Thank you Jesus," she cried, "Thank you Jesus!"

Police Officer Alexander radioed into headquarters of his findings as he was trained to do whenever he observed something strange or unusual. He described a woman nicely dressed and a young boy in pajamas walking on the interstate at 5:50 AM, which certainly appeared to be strange. "There are no abandoned cars anywhere in sight and they are on a major interstate walking! Where are they going or coming from?" he thought. Teresa quickly pulled Jamie closer to her side as Officer Alexander got out of his patrol car.

"Ma'm, are you okay?" he asked.

"No Sir, we had been kidnapped and tied up in a shack and we just got free. Please help us!" she cried, trying to control her voice and hysteria.

"Okay, just slow down and let's get in the car and out of danger. Too many cars and trucks are zooming by and it is a bit hard to hear. Okay?" Teresa nodded in agreement.

Officer Alexander opened the door to the patrol car and seated them in the back seat.

"Okay, now first, let's get your name and address and I will take your statement. I would prefer to take you to the precinct to take your statement but before we go there, do you need medical attention?"

"No, we are fine."

"Kidnapping is a felony and there must be charges filed against this person. I know this has been a terrible ordeal for you Ms..."

"Hayward, Teresa Hayward and this is my son Jamie," she interjected.

"Okay, Ms. Hayward. Tell me exactly what happened. I will take your statement when I get you to the precinct. But in the meantime, can you show me where you and your son were taken and tied up?"

"Yes, I can show you." They soon turned down the dirt road and Jamie became more talkative.

He told the officer that he knew where he was, because he and Ricky went fishing there. When they arrived at the shack, the candle was still burning. Officer Alexander blew out the candle and looked around. He went back to the patrol car to get his camera. He took pictures of the chair that still had the restraints tied to the slats as well as the candle and the rest of the meager contents in the dilapidated one room shack.

Teresa was mentally and physically exhausted when they finally arrived at the police station. As she told the story to Officer Alexander, she would spell out certain things so as not to upset Jamie. In her mind she was so upset about allowing herself to fall in love with such a dangerous man. She marveled at her own naiveté. She was livid that she allowed such a man to also become so close to her son Jamie. She could not stop crying. She was still crying when Chief Lee came into the holding room and asked to speak to Officer Alexander in his office.

"I will be right back Ms. Hayward," he said.

Jamie stood by his mother, trying to wipe away her tears. He kept hugging her and telling her that everything was going to be alright when Ricky comes.

"Momma you have to call Ricky and let him know we are safe now. He went to get the bad guys that are at our house." Teresa did not know what to say to Jamie. She did not know how to tell him that Ricky *was* the bad guy. She nodded her head as he wiped at her tears.

Officer Alexander returned a few minutes later.

"Teresa Hayward, I am sorry but we are going to have to detain you here. Is there a family member you can call to come get your son?"

"What? What are you talking about? Detain me, for what?" Teresa's brown eyes widened as she stood up, not able to comprehend what he was saying.

"I was just informed that we have reason to believe that you were involved in drug smuggling at Paradise Pillows with Ricky Clay. You will be detained until a more thorough investigation is done. There could be more charges against you. I am sorry but you need to call someone to come get your son. You can make one call. Make it count."

Teresa sat speechless and numb for a second. She was trying hard to understand what he was actually saying. She began to repeat out loud what he had just said. "No, this is not happening. This is a dream right? I need to wake up now!" She began to pat Jamie's face and head to see if he was real. Jamie pulled away not understanding what she was doing.

"Ms. Hayward, you need to make a call for a family member to come get your son, or I will have to call Child Protective Service."

Teresa snapped her head around in disbelief.

"Please sir, there must be some mistake. I have no idea as to what you are talking about," she pleaded.

"You need to make the call or not? I am doing my job and right now lady, you are under arrest and I will be taking you to be fingerprinted, photographed and then to your holding cell. My last time asking ... Do you want to call a family member?" He asked, yet again, trying to not show his frustration. He had gotten orders from Chief Lee to let her make a call so someone could come and get her son and she is not cooperating. Otherwise it would have been to hold her like everyone else for 48 hours with no calls to anyone. Chief wanted to make sure no one got tipped off about the bust.

"Yes, please call Ms. Joni King." He scribbled the number she recited down on a pad he took from his shirt pocket. "Thank you," she said, looking at Jamie who looked really confused now.

"Jamie, Momma King is coming to get you and I want you to be brave and a big guy for me. I may have to stay here for a day or so. There has been a mistake and I have to stay here until it is straightened out, okay?'

"Yes, Momma, but when will you come and get me from Momma King?"

"Hopefully later on today or tomorrow, okay?"

"Okay Momma. I love you, and, Momma, don't forget to say your prayers, okay?" Teresa smiled and kissed him and held him tightly to her chest. He was everything she had.

"Oh God, please fix this mess I am in. Please help me Jesus," she prayed silently.

Teresa had only a few minutes to elucidate about what had happened but she was not sure herself. She focused on what the arresting officer had said as she tried to relay the information to Momma King.

"They said they have reason to believe that I am involved in drug trafficking with Ricky," Teresa said quivering.

Ms. King asked, "Did they arrest Ricky too?"

"No," she said. "He kidnapped me and Jamie last night and left us in a shack on the outskirts of town." Teresa had no way of knowing that Ricky was arrested right after he left them tied up in the shack. The police did not inform her about having Ricky in their custody as well. "We managed to get untied and were walking back into the city early this morning when the police stopped us. I told them what happened and they brought me here and now they are saying I was involved somehow with Ricky smuggling drugs through the warehouse at Paradise!" Teresa sobbed.

"I am on my way. See you in a few minutes." Ms. King hung up and was there in less than ten minutes. Teresa was so relieved to see her.

Ms. King took charge of the situation. "Okay, listen. I will contact my attorney and I will be back as soon as I can. Don't worry. I saw you and Jamie in a vision last night. You both were in an old dilapidated shack. The vision occurred shortly after you left. I tried to call you but there was no answer. As I began to pray for you and Jamie, the Peace of God settled upon me and I knew that whatever was happening, you and Jamie were going to be alright. Now don't you fret my child. God is with you and we are gonna get you out of this mess. I am so sorry you and Jamie had to go through that, but everything is going to be fine now, okay? I will ..."

"Sorry, but we have to book you now," Officer Alexander said interrupting.

"Ms. King, please go now and thanks for taking care of Jamie." She tried to smile.

Ms. King realized that Teresa did not want Jamie to see the police put her in handcuffs.

Teresa was petrified as she was fingerprinted, photographed and put in a cold empty jail cell. She gagged from the stench of the toilet as she sat on the edge of the cot that was visibly filthy. She watched as the guard locked the steel bars, leaving her all alone.

CHAPTER 44

Billy and Dante did not bother to get undressed. They both were exhausted. It had been a long day. Sitting upright with their heads propped on a pillow at the opposite ends of the couch, they fell asleep hoping that Ricky would come in and wake them up. Dante woke first and shook Billy awake. "Hey Man, get up. Ricky never came home! Man, we have been double-crossed! He took all the money for himself! He is a dead man! I am going to track him and his girl Teresa down if that is the last thing I do! Let's go to the warehouse and see if there is any kind of action there!" Dante stormed, flexing his muscles. "He better not be anywhere in sight! He is as good as dead!"

"Hey Dante, let's not jump to conclusions yet. Anything could have happened. We need to go over what we know for sure. Rick knew we were coming and was planning to meet us here early in the evening after he got off from work. Looking at the contents of what he had in the refrigerator, it appears like he was intending to celebrate with us. He did not call either of us. We went to The Oasis Nightclub. We could not find him or Big Mc, and no one had seen them all evening. Don't you find that unusual Dante?" Not waiting for an answer, he continued,

"We go to his girl's house and no one is there and it appeared someone left in a rush. Some clothes were hanging out of the dresser drawers. Her purse was on the couch with a few dollars and a set of keys on a chair nearby."

Dante added, "Yeah, it could have been staged to make us think something like that happened. Rick could want us to think they both had been kidnapped or something. There is no money and no Rick! I don't want to think anymore! Let's go find some answers, but first I want to check Rick's closet for the spare handgun he always kept in his shoe box!"

"Wait Dante, let's not take it now. Let's go check out the warehouse. If we don't find any answers, then we will know something is definitely wrong. Then let's get 'armed up' okay? And besides, it's Saturday morning and only a few of the drivers will be there, if anyone is there at all."

Billy was always the more reasonable and sensible one. He did not want Dante with a gun especially if there was a possibility that he might see Rick. And seeing how mad Dante was, Billy did not want to take any chances.

"Okay Man...Okay. No guns for now! "Dante yelled back, "Let's go!"

They found the warehouse rather easily. There were several cars nearby, but no one was in the warehouse or the office. There was no sight of Rick or his car. For over an hour, they sat and watched the warehouse.

During that same hour, Agent Haddon and Agent Marcos sat and watched them and the warehouse (from their unmarked police car) which had been under surveillance since Nate had been hospitalized. Dante and Billy argued with each other, not knowing what to do next. Did Ricky really double-cross them, they wondered. Just as they decided to leave, Sal drove into the parking lot near the warehouse.

Sal was excited to get back to work and decided to swing by the warehouse to see if Ricky had a delivery set up for him to do on Monday. He also wanted to talk to Ricky about his experience in the Poconos and about Ricky's relationship with God. Sal reflected back to when Ricky cried as he was told about his relationship with God, his abuse as a child, and how he had disrespected his wife. Sal had never seen the warehouse so deserted. Even though it was Saturday and not a regular work day, there was usually a small amount of activity in the warehouse. There were no trucks visible, no one in the office, no one anywhere. It just seemed too quiet.

Billy and Dante watched Sal check the doors to the warehouse. They both were locked. Ricky had never given him a key to the warehouse. Puzzled and perplexed, Sal went back to his car and drove away. At the end of the road, Detective Dudley stopped him and flashed his badge. Detective Dudley spoke very precisely and had a heavy bass voice. He was dressed in dark tan khakis with a light blue shirt, and was clean shaven, with a slightly receding hairline. He recognized Sal from one of the photos taken as the driver of the van in Florida with the name *Paradise* on the door and New York license plates, which was believed to have been transporting drugs.

"I stopped you because I need to know, what is your business here at Paradise Pillows?"

"I work here. I am one of their drivers," Sal answered.

"I need to see some identification, please," Detective Dudley requested.

"Sure," reaching for his wallet and removing his driver's license. Sal handed it to him.

"Stay put. I will be right back." Detective Dudley entered Sal's information into the nation-wide data base. It came back clean. Not even a parking ticket. "Sal Tully, I need you to come downtown to answer a few questions at the police station."

Alarmed, Sal asked, "For what? Why is it that I need to go to the police station?"

"We have reason to believe you are involved in transporting drugs up and down the east coast."

"Drugs? Is this some kind of joke?"

"No, this is not a joke. We need you to come downtown now."

Reluctantly Sal parked his car and went with the detective in the unmarked car. In a state of shock and disbelief, Sal insisted they had made a mistake. Detective Dudley took Sal into a small room painted white, which contained a dark brown wooden table and three chairs chained to the floor. Sal had never been in trouble with the law before and was visibly shaking. He gladly welcomed the chair because his legs were weak and he felt sick. "How did I get into this predicament? Drugs?" He gagged at the thought of it and of sharing this unbelievable mistake with Carolyn.

They were soon joined by Police Chief Lee, who actually did most of the interrogation. It did not feel like questions were being asked of him. It felt more like they were telling Sal what he did. It was all the more confusing to Sal when they showed him a picture of himself in the company's van, making a delivery in Florida.

Sal continued to deny knowledge of any drugs. He explained over and over again that he started to work for the company only a few months earlier, having been offered a job to deliver pillows to various hubs along the east coast by Ricky Clay. "I never asked questions because as far as I knew, I was delivering pillows," he said. Sal never deviated from his story.

Police Chief Lee left the room and returned two hours later. He had driven over to the hotel to see Nate Bishop to validate some of the information Sal had told him. Detective Dudley carried on with the interrogation. After being grilled over and over again for nearly two hours, Chief Lee entered the small room again and took a seat.

"Anything new Detective Dudley?" Chief Lee asked.

"No, he is still sticking to his story and insists that I call Ricky Clay."

"Okay Sal, since we only have a picture of you driving, we can't hold you or charge you with drug smuggling, so we are going to release you now, but don't leave the city or the country until our investigation is complete. And don't talk to anyone about this interrogation. Do you understand?"

Sal was speechless and nodded his head, waiting for his next instruction.

"Okay, you can leave now. Detective Dudley will drive you back to your car."

"No, that is okay. I think I will walk. I need to clear my head." Sal could not believe what had just happened to him. His mind raced, "Where is Ricky Clay? Did the police arrest him or question him? Did he set me up to deliver drugs? No, Rick is a good guy. If it weren't for him, I would not have a job. No, there must be a big mistake. I am sure this will be all cleared up by Monday and all will be back to business as usual."

His thoughts continued, "I told Leslie to let Rick know I was back and would be back to work on Monday but if he needed me before Monday, to call me. The detective could not have been there for me, because I was not scheduled to be there. Something is going on and it must be pretty big to have Paradise Pillows staked out. Should I tell Carolyn what just happened?" Interrupting himself, he answered out loud talking to himself. "Yes, of course I will tell her, she is my wife. We can't have secrets if our marriage is going to stay strong and healthy. We just spent a few days in the Poconos re-establishing our love and commitment to each other. Yes, I will tell her everything as soon as I get home."

****

Ms. King tried earnestly to contact her attorney most of Saturday morning. Unable to reach him, she called Pastor Sherman to ask if he were free to go with her to the police station to encourage Teresa. She shared with him as much as she knew, which was not very much.

"Sure," he said, "I will be there in about an hour. Should I meet you there or should I pick you up?"

"Well actually, I am waiting for Sister Shironi to come here to stay with Jamie. He is so worried about his momma. They are extremely close. He has been crying. He doesn't understand why the police are keeping her. So, when Sister Shironi comes, I will pick you up and we can go together. She will be here in a half an hour." Mother King responded.

"Okay, that will be great," he said.

"Oh, Pastor, do you know a good criminal attorney? I have been trying to reach mine all day but to no avail. He is probably out of town, and I need to get a good one to help Teresa."

"Yes, sure. I have a friend who is a criminal attorney and one of the best in the area. I use him from time to time if some of my people at church are in need of legal advice. Let me see if I can reach him. Do you want him to come today with us?"

"Yes, that would be great. Thank you so much Pastor Sherman. I will call you when I am on my way. Oh, just ask your attorney friend to meet us at the police station in about an hour if he can. I will get his name and number later."

"Okay, see you in a bit."

CHAPTER 45

Teresa was in deep thought. Her eyes were inflamed from crying. She was trying to make sense of her situation, when she suddenly heard Momma King's voice. She was overwhelmed with joy and tried to wipe the tears from her eyes. "Perhaps she is here to get me out of this horrible jail cell," she thought. Teresa raced to the cell bars and peered down the corridor as far as she could, trying to see Momma King. The attending police officer stepped from around the corner and over to the jail cell with a key and unlocked the door. "Uh, Teresa Hayward, you have a few visitors." Happy, humiliated, and fearful all at the same time, she rushed to Momma King, hugged her and cried tears of relief. She was suddenly feeling safe for the moment as Momma King hugged her back.

"Teresa, you remember Pastor Sherman, right?"

Smiling shyly Teresa extended her hand, "Yes, Pastor Sherman, it is nice to see you again," she said.

"And this is Troy Kennedy. He is your attorney." Again, Teresa smiled shyly and shook his hand. Troy looked deeply into her eyes and said, "Now, don't you worry young lady. We are going to do our best to get to the bottom of this ordeal, but you must be open and honest with me and tell me everything... from the very beginning." The attending police officer motioned them to the visitation room at the end of the corridor. They were quickly seated around the metal table.

Troy appeared to be in his late thirties with pearly white teeth and a dazzling smile. His dark brown eyes were intense and his mannerism was very comforting. He was very easy to talk to. Teresa poured out her heart about everything she knew regarding Ricky Clay. She explained how he was loved by everyone at Paradise and how she had met him in high school and quickly fell in love with him when he was hired at Paradise as a maintenance technician. She continued on about how he quickly gained the love and respect of his co-workers and especially Nate Bishop, who was impressed with his ability to increase the sales for the company in a very short period of time. She recalled the day she heard the loud voices coming from Nate's office and saw Ricky with a gun to Nate's head. Then about how Nate collapsed and suffered a major stroke. She told of her part in calling the ambulance and pretending to Ricky that she did not see anything, which was the first time she became fearful of him. She shared about Ricky's relationship with Jamie; the time they spent together fishing and his wanting to take care of Jamie and opening a savings account for him. Trying to compose herself from time to time, her inflamed eyes burned as she suddenly remembered the pain of his accusations. She recalled Ricky punching her in the head, knocking her out, and tying her up. She remembered everything including the dilapidated shack she and Jamie escaped from earlier that morning. Chills ran through her body, causing her to shake uncontrollably.

Several times Momma King put her arms around her, comforting and encouraging her to go on. Teresa shared how Ricky asked her to make labels for things he wanted to ship to his friends, the reason being to clearly differentiate his boxes from those of the company. She stated how she never gave it any thought until last week when Nate Bishop asked her about the labels and she informed him that it was she who made them. Nate had been disappointed that she had not told him about it. He then had asked her not to say anything to Ricky. Pausing a minute, Troy asked, "Did you tell Ricky?"

"No, I never said anything to him. I became afraid for me and Jamie and I decided to change the locks at my apartment."

Momma King's eyes were now filled with tears, "Oh my poor child! Why you didn't tell me?"

Teresa said, "I did not know how. I almost told you last week when I spent the night with you. You were so right Momma King. I am so sorry I did not listen to you. Now I am in jail accused of drug trafficking! Please, get me out of here," she cried as she turned to Troy. He was writing on a steno pad that had plenty of notes.

"Oh, it is going to be okay child. God is going to deliver you. Don't you worry," encouraged Momma King.

Troy added, "Yes, Teresa, I am going to do my very best, but due to the fact that this is Saturday, you must stay here until Monday when the judge comes in. I will speak to the judge on your behalf and I will meet you in court on Monday morning at 9 AM.

"NO!, NO! Please get me out of here now!!!" Teresa became hysterical and the attending police officer came quickly to the room.

"Is everything okay?" he asked. "Yes," Pastor Sherman spoke up. "Yes, we are getting ready to pray now."

The attending police officer nodded his head. "Just give me a call when you are ready to leave."

Momma King tried her best to console Teresa, but she was out of control, screaming and yelling. Pastor Sherman touched her forehead and said *"Peace, I speak Peace to your spirit, now, In Jesus Name."* Teresa immediately began to calm down. Momma King joined in and soon they were all praying and praising God...even Teresa. After Teresa had regained her composure, Troy said, "I have just one more question. Do I have your permission to ask Jamie a few questions?"

"No, please don't involve my son. He is just a child." she pleaded.

"Well if this should go to trial, he will be subpoenaed and then he must answer all questions. I am hoping to get enough information from him to establish a believable defense so that we won't have to go to trial. It is imperative that we get his statement, especially about what happened when you were unconscious and then awoke in the shack. Jamie's statement could be very vital and key in your case."

Ms. King implored, "Let him speak to Jamie and get his account of what happened so there are no holes in your story. I will be with him to assure him everything will be fine, and to just tell what happened the night you were kidnapped. Let us help."

"Okay," she relented, "but Momma King, will you promise to look after Jamie?"

"Of course I will child, but you will be home soon to look after him yourself. Have faith in God. Be strong and stop crying," she said, kissing her on the forehead.

CHAPTER 46

Dante and Billy noticed the two unmarked police cars as they left the parking lot of Paradise Pillows. Seeing the police cars, they were now convinced that something had happened and either the police were looking for Ricky or they had him in their possession. Unsure as to what to do next, they decided to drive back over to Teresa's apartment. Everything looked exactly the same as it had been the night before. They decided to go to The Oasis to see if anyone had seen Big Mc. Again, no one had seen him and all seemed unusually quiet.

Billy suggested, "Hey Man, let's go back to Ricky's apartment and lay low until we figure out what to do next. I have a strong feeling that the police have Ricky in their custody. It makes sense. The warehouse is being staked out and the question is, why? It is probably being watched because they are trying to find out who is working with Ricky. Man, I think we should get out of here."

"Naw, Man you may be right. If you are right, we can't leave now. I have an idea. How about we go to the police station and report Ricky as a missing person. It has been over twenty-four hours. This idea might answer a lot of questions for us. Whatcha think?" Dante said, smiling brilliantly.

Billy hesitated to answer right away. He was very careful in his thought process. "Well, the only problem I have with that plan is the police will want to know who we are if we report him as missing. They will begin asking us a lot of questions and then perhaps snoop around his apartment. We don't want that kind of attention. How about this idea? If Ricky is in jail, then he will be allowed to make one phone call right?" Not waiting for Dante's answer, he continued. "So, if you have one phone call to make, who would he call that he could trust?

"Us?" Dante said.

"Right!" Billy said, "But since we did not receive a call, who would be the next person he would call?"

"An attorney," Dante said, guessing but not really sure if he answered correctly.

"Yes! We can go to the police station as his attorney. If he is there, they will have to let us in to see him. If he is not there, we can pretend it was a mistake. But then we will know for sure he betrayed us," Billy explained.

"Brilliant Billy, that's brilliant Man."

"Let's go back to Ricky's and change clothes. We have to look the part." Suddenly feeling inspired by the idea, they were confident that they would have some answers soon.

After changing clothes and going over their plan, they arrived at the police station. Billy posed as the lawyer and Dante as his legal assistant. They approached a police officer who appeared to be pre-occupied with some files on his desk. "Uh, excuse me Officer. I am Billy Mason, and this is my legal assistant, Dante Williams. We are here to see my client, Mr. Ricky Clay." Officer Lawrence looked up over his glasses through the half-barred steel enclosure at the two standing before him.

"What's the name?"

"Ricky Clay"

"Oh, just a minute. Let me check. May I see your identification please?"

"Sure," Billy answered. He and Dante took out their driver's licenses and gave them to him. Officer Lawrence went into the back of the office, leaving the two alone in the empty lobby. They laughed and winked at each other as if they had successfully cracked the code to a bank vault.

Officer Lawrence went directly to Chief Lee's office.

"Chief Lee, didn't we have a *48 Hour No Call* on Ricky Clay?

"Yes, Lawrence, we do. Why did you ask?"

"Well Sir, there are two men in the lobby here to see him saying they are his attorney."

"Really? You have their ID?" Chief inquired.

"Yes sir" laying them both on his desk.

"Okay, quickly run their names through the nation-wide data base. We don't want them to become suspicious. They are probably a part of his drug connection wondering what happened to him and the money. There is no way they could know Ricky Clay is here, unless we have an informant here on the inside," Chief Lee said.

"Sure thing, Chief."

Officer Lawrence was back within a few minutes with the information on both men, Billy and Dante.

"Yes, Chief, They are definitely linked together. They have all been arrested before together. They have quite a history together."

Chief looked over the report and remembered a bank account opened by Ricky Clay in the name of Reverend Dante according to the information Agents Haddon and Marco reported from the bank manager, Mr. Wenzel. "Could this be the same person?" he thought.

"Yes, this is the same address on the license he gave us and it also matches the bank account that was opened in Jamie's name. Billy Mason's name is also on one of the accounts opened in Teresa Hayward's name," Chief confirmed.

"BINGO!!! We have two more pieces of the missing links. Get a couple of fellow officers to go out there and arrest them both. I will contact the Federal Bureau of Investigation (FBI) since they have crossed state lines. This is a federal case now. Make sure they get some legal representation before Monday when they have to go to court. Hopefully this bust will be a great headline for the newspaper and the precinct. I am so proud of you all and your hard work! You are making me look good as your new Chief of Police! Be sure they do not see Ricky, Big

Mc or Teresa. We still have some investigating to do and I don't want them to know those others have been arrested," Chief Lee said smiling. "I think Teresa Hayward was being used unknowingly in assisting Ricky Clay. She seems quite frightened and naive. But let's see what comes out on Monday," he said. "She will learn a good lesson sitting there in that jail cell."

Two more police officers came out with Officer Lawrence. They moved from behind the enclosed barred steel enclosure out into the lobby. Dante and Billy's hearts sank.

"Uh-oh, Dante, I don't think this was a good idea," Billy mumbled.

"Dante Williams and Billy Mason, you both are being detained for further investigation for your involvement in drug smuggling and impersonating an attorney; which , by the way, you will probably be needing one... a real good one too," Officer Lawrence snickered.

A fellow officer handcuffed them and took them in the back to be processed. They surrendered quietly and without incident.

"No need to finger print them. They are already in the system," Officer Lawrence told his fellow officers. "Chief Lee wants them held here until Monday morning, when they will then go before the Honorable Judge Les Harris."

CHAPTER 47

Esq. Troy Kennedy never married after his fiancée had broken off their engagement while he was pursuing his Masters in Business Law. They met their first year in college at Harvard University. Patty, his fiancée, was interested in becoming a lawyer as well. She lost sight of her goals and ambition when her mother died suddenly from pneumonia. Grief and anger had consumed her and she was no longer able to focus on her school work. She eventually left school and got a job in their local home town and hung out with her friends and saw Troy when he could. She was constantly complaining that she wanted more of Troy's time, but seemed emotionally disconnected from him. He still loved her and tried to get help for her. Patty insisted she was fine and refused to go to a professional to get help in dealing with her grief. Troy promised her the world, but she did not care and continued on a downward spiral, experimenting with drugs and pills to numb the pain.

Two years before he passed the bar to become a lawyer, she gave him back his two carat diamond ring. He was devastated at the time, but in hindsight he knew it was a blessing from God. They were no longer compatible and were on two different paths. He realized it never would have worked. She was very high maintenance, very self centered and sometimes even delusional. He, on the other hand, worked extremely hard, managed his money very well and was determined to make a reputation for himself as the best criminal attorney in the area. He eventually secured an unbeatable reputation for winning every case that came to him. He was an excellent attorney who was highly recommended by all of his colleagues. He never really took time to pursue a meaningful relationship after the breakup with Patty. It was always work first and foremost, until he met Teresa.

"She is different and definitely worth pursuing," he thought. "But first things first. I must win back her freedom." He never felt so connected to any of his clients as he was with Teresa Hayward. She was very beautiful and her eyes haunted him. They were sad and intriguing all at the same time. Troy decided he would take a trip back to the police station to talk to Chief Lee and visit with Teresa the next day after church. He spent all of Saturday evening and late into the early hours of the morning going over his notes and making a list of questions to add clarity. He was intent on making sure he could defend her properly and bring her comfort while she was there as well as to go over every detail of her involvement with Ricky Clay. He wanted to know everything; everything about everything.

CHAPTER 48

Ricky Clay had been pacing back and forth all day in his tiny jail cell, trying to sort things out in his mind. He replayed the events of all that had happened. It suddenly dawned on him that the man who had come into Paradise to order the bulk of pillows was the same man who had arrested him! "Agent Marco!! Yes, that is why his face looked so familiar. It was a set up. But why would he pretend to order pillows? He was distracting me from something, but what?" he wondered. All of a sudden it became very clear. "He distracted me long enough for his partner to take the money from the trunk of my car. Yes, that's it! He took it!" he yelled out loud, feeling relieved at knowing the answer to the mystery.

He then became consumed with guilt thinking of Teresa tied up in the shack and the fact that he actually hit her. He had convinced Jamie to leave his mother tied until he returned to get them. "How could I have been such a monster?" he acknowledged. "How could I have hurt Teresa and accuse her of stealing the money?" His heart was throbbing with pain and guilt. It was at that moment, that Ricky realized he truly loved her and Jamie.

Officer Guadalupe had just passed by his jail cell. Overwhelmed, Ricky cried out to him, "please come here, I have a confession to make. There are some innocent people who may be in trouble. Please help them." Surprised by Ricky's emotional outburst, Officer Guadalupe slowly approached Ricky's cell. He motioned to the guard seated at the end of the hall to come join him.

"Please, you have to help them!!" Ricky screamed.

"Who needs help?" Officer Guadalupe asked.

"My girlfriend and her son! I left them in the old abandoned shack on the outskirts of town, by the fishing pond. Her name is Teresa Hayward and her son is Jamie. I thought she stole money from me and I took her there to scare her into confessing where she hid my money. It is all my fault! I realize now that she doesn't know anything! Please go get them! Please, they have been there since last night!" he pleaded.

Officer Guadalupe said, "Okay, we will take care of it. Just calm down. I will be right back." He quickly went to Chief Lee's office. Chief Lee was just leaving to go home for the evening.

"I am so glad I caught you."

"Why, what's going on?" Chief inquired.

"Ricky Clay just made a confession that he had tied up his girlfriend and her son in the old abandoned shack on the outskirts of town. He said he thought she had stolen his money but now claims she had nothing to do with anything and he wants us to go get her and her son," Officer Guadalupe explained. "What should I do? Do I let him know we already picked her up and she is in the east wing jail cell, just opposite him and the rest of his cronies?"

"No, just let him know we will get her and her son. Don't tell him we are already holding her. I just spoke with Sal Tully, who is a driver for Paradise Pillows and also Nate Bishop. They both are convinced Teresa is not involved in any way, but only made labels for Ricky. She obviously did not know what he was doing with them. We interrogated Sal Tully about his involvement and we are convinced he too was being used as a driver and had no knowledge of anything else. So, since it is getting late now, I am going to keep her locked up until she appears before the judge on Monday with the rest of them. Hopefully she will learn a valuable lesson from all of this. I spoke to Judge Les Harris. He already knows her situation."

Ricky collapsed to his knees when Officer Guadalupe told him a car was sent out to get them. Ricky continued to cry and did not even realize he was praising God and giving Him thanks. He felt so relieved to know that she and Jamie would be safe. He called on the Name of Jesus, unashamed and uncaring as to who heard him.

"Please forgive me Jesus!" he repeated. He cried and thanked God so much that he thought he was delusional when he heard a language coming out of his mouth he had never heard or known before.

"What is this? What has happened to me?" he thought, in the midst of his transformation. The more Ricky cried and praised God the happier he felt and the more the heavenly language flowed out of his innermost being. He only cared about the moment he was currently experiencing. Nothing and no one else seemed to matter. There was such joy and peace in his soul which he never knew could be possible.

Officer Herring came down the hall and witnessed the conversion and began to praise God with Ricky. They talked a long time afterwards about God and this new *born-again* experience. He told Ricky he did not know how his ordeal would turn out for him, but said, "If by some miracle you are released, please come to my church, Light of Love Ministries and meet my pastor, Pastor W. Dale Sherman." Ricky was surprised to hear the name of his church and the pastor. It was the same church Big Mc told him he visited from time to time when he was overwhelmed with his sinful lifestyle.

"Yes," Ricky said. "I will. I have heard about your church. Maybe one day Man, maybe one day," as reality set in that he was no longer a free man. He suddenly became aware of being a free man spiritually, but realized he was not a free man physically. He was incarcerated for drug trafficking and now for kidnapping, assault and endangering the welfare of a child. If found guilty, he knew he could possibly spend the rest of his life behind bars. Maybe God would be merciful to him somehow. At least he now knew he has a heart and can feel love and compassion for someone other than himself. He thought of Teresa and Jamie in the old shack and said a prayer for them and their safety. He prayed that Teresa would somehow find it in her heart to forgive him and to not hate him. Ricky later fell asleep giving thanks to God and, for the first time since he could remember, he was content and slept soundly without any interruptions.

CHAPTER 49

Sunday morning was cloudy and looked as if it were going to rain. Just as Ms. King and Jamie were walking out the door, she turned back to get her umbrella, and the phone rang.

"Hello" said Ms. King.

"Hello, Ms. King, this is Troy Kennedy. I just wanted you to know I am going to spend the day with Teresa to make sure I did not miss anything. I am going to do everything possible to prove her innocence. I got quite a bit of information from Jamie yesterday and I appreciate your help, but is there anything else I need to know that perhaps you can tell me?"

"Actually no, I can't think of anything at the moment, but Jamie and I are on our way to church. If I think of anything I will call you when I get back in from church. I am very pleased to have you represent her, Mr. Kennedy. I have a real peace about this whole thing. It is in God's Hands and I trust Him with Teresa. She and Jamie are just like my own flesh and blood. Jamie is very worried about his Momma. Well, since you are going there today, please let her know I will be there on Monday after I put

Jamie on the bus. I wanted to visit with her after church, but I don't have anyone to stay with Jamie. So I am glad you are going to be there with her. She is so afraid."

"Yes, Ms. King, I know. Her eyes haunted me all night. Tell Jamie I am working very hard to make sure his Mommy comes home soon. Have a great time in church and of course pray for us all."

"Okay, I will and thanks so much for calling. Give me a call later when you leave the police station and let me know how she is doing okay?

"Yes of course, I will give you a call later. God bless you."

"Thanks and God bless you too Mr. Kennedy. Good bye."

Ms. King smiled at his commitment and determination to prove Teresa's innocence. She did not notice Jamie watching every expression on her face. He was waiting eagerly to hear about his momma. Jamie tugged at the pocketbook she was clutching tightly to get her attention.

"Is my momma coming to church with us today?"

"No Sweetie, but we will continue to pray that God will allow her to come home real soon, okay?"

Jamie looked as if he were going to cry. Momma King quickly pulled him to her bosom and reassured him that everything was going to be fine. "We will say a special prayer for your momma today in church and we need you to be a big boy, okay?"

Jamie nodded his head and pulled away. He wanted to be a big boy, remembering Ricky telling him to be "the Man" when he left him in the shack.

"I am a big boy" he said, and opened the door for Ms. King. "Ricky said I will soon be a man like him."

"Why yes, of course," she replied, trying not to show her frustration. "Hummph," she grunted. "Surely Teresa will have to tell Jamie about the *real* Ricky," she thought.

They arrived at church and found it full to capacity. She and Jamie sat up in the balcony, which was most unusual for a rainy Sunday morning service. There were many new faces that filled the thousand seat edifice. It was very obvious that those who came for the Young Adult Sharing the Power Program felt the presence of God and experienced a life changing moment. The word had traveled quickly in the little community and many had come out to see and to experience the presence of God for themselves. Ms. King was very pleased. It was a glorious gathering indeed. Ms. King loved her seat in the balcony because she could see everybody. "Oh, there's Margie and Shironi sitting together. Praise God she came back and it looks like she may have brought some friends," she smiled with approval.

Pastor Sherman took the microphone and thanked everyone for coming out. He shared that he sensed the presence of the Holy Spirit in a deep strong way that morning. "Don't be shy today. You are here for a purpose. God has the plan and purpose for your life. It is a good plan, even if you are hurting today. His plan for you is still good."

He turned to the choir and they stood up in unison. He began to sing and they all joined in with uplifted hands. They sang with such love and sincerity:

"Welcome Holy Spirit,

We are in your presence,

fill us with your power, live inside of us.

You are the Alpha and Omega

The beginning and the end, with a plan for our lives,

come take complete control.

Welcome Holy Spirit..."

They sang for several minutes and the people's faith began to rise and the Shekinah Glory filled the church. It looked like a mist of white smoke lingering in the atmosphere. It was normal to see fog outside because it was raining, but here it was foggy *inside* the church. The presence of God filled the temple just as it was written in 2 Chronicles 5:13... "And when they lifted up their voice with the trumpets and cymbals and instruments of music, and praised the Lord, saying, for He is Good; for His Mercy endureth forever: then the house was filled with a cloud, even the house of the Lord." Ms. King saw the cloud of smoke and was in awe of the presence of God. As she worshipped God, she thought of Teresa and sensed a peace and a joy deep within her soul. She knew God was working everything out for Teresa. She remembered the scripture that God lead her to read last night before going to bed while praying for Teresa. It was Psalms 138:8, "*The Lord will perfect that which concerns me; Your mercy, O Lord, endures forever; do not forsake the works of Your hands.*"

The church was charged with an illumination that seemed to be on each person who was assembled. It was electric!

Ms. King loved how Pastor Sherman seemed to flow with whatever the Holy Spirit wanted to do on each particular Sunday. There had been some occasions when he did not preach at all. In those times the gifts of the Holy Spirit would minister in songs, prophecy or words of knowledge for the entirety of the service. People would be healed, delivered and encouraged. There would be a sweet gentle loving Spirit flowing from heart to heart, to everyone and anyone who was open to the presence of God. Sometimes there would be dancing, laughing, weeping, and hugging throughout the service, always with freedom and liberty. Many times there would be testimonies of healing, restoration and answered prayers.

Jamie was enthralled as they made their way down to the altar. Mother King held Jamie's hand and agreed with him in prayer. He again felt the presence of God run over his body like hot oil just as he had felt at Momma King's house when she had prayed and anointed him with oil. He could not hold back the tears as he prayed for his momma to come home. His faith was ginormous! He really believed God was going to bring his momma home to him.

The three hour church service had ended but many were still lingering around when Ms. King heard her name being called. "Mother King, Mother King!" It was Shironi and Margie and another couple that Ms. King did not recognize. Mother King smiled and hugged them all.

"So good to see you again Shironi and Margie," she exclaimed.

"Yes, I loved the fellowship so much last Friday night, that I invited my neighbors, Sal and Carolyn Tully." She paused while they acknowledged each other again.

Shironi was bubbling over with joy and quickly interjected, "Yes, Sal and Carolyn are new believers and will be coming here to fellowship. I am trying to get Sal to join the choir. He has a deep baritone voice that is unbelievable. I heard him singing this morning." Sal blushed and looked to Carolyn to somehow rescue him. Carolyn agreed wholeheartedly. Margie and Carolyn giggled at Sal's discomfort.

"Well, it is so nice to see you all again. Don't forget we have an awesome Bible Study on Wednesday night at 7 PM. Please come if you can," Mother King added.

CHAPTER 50

It was in the early evening on Sunday when Troy Kennedy stopped by to see Ms. King. Surprised to see him she asked, "Did I misunderstand? I thought you were going to call me after the visit." She did not want to call Teresa by name, not wanting Jamie to hear. Troy quickly understood and answered, "Yes, you are right I was supposed to call but I really wanted to talk to you in person. If this is not a good time, we can talk a little later this evening if you don't mind."

"No, it is fine. Is she okay?" Ms. King inquired.

"As much as can be expected," he said sadly.

"Excuse me Troy for one minute. Let me check on Jamie and tuck him into bed. He was just brushing his teeth. Please make yourself comfortable and help yourself to some tea or coffee," as she pointed toward the kitchen. "Everything is there. Just help yourself," she yelled from the other room.

"Oh okay, sure. Thanks so much and take your time. I should have called first," he said feeling a bit guilty. It was almost 9 PM when Troy Kennedy left. He learned so much about Teresa from Ms. King's perspective and earlier from Teresa's own account of herself and Jamie. He learned of her abandonment by her mother when she was ten years old. Her mother, Lena, had run off with a man who claimed was going to make her into a professional model and movie star. Lena left Teresa with her mother Clara Mae promising she would be back in six months. Teresa only heard from her mother the first two years of her absence on her birthday and once on Christmas and then never again. Those times she would always promise Teresa that she would be back for her soon. Five years later, the day Teresa turned seventeen years old, Grandma Lena passed away suddenly from a massive heart attack. Since Teresa was not of age to live on her own legally, and the courts could not find her mother, she was placed in a foster home. It was there, her mental state of rejection was compounded with verbal abuse by her foster parents.

Teresa became very shy and had very low self esteem. She stayed away from home as much as possible. It was never a place where she felt loved or wanted. She felt like her foster parents treated her like a slave and someone of very little importance. One time she recalled her foster father had tried to rape her. He slipped into the bathroom while she was showering, and grabbed her from behind and covered her mouth. Teresa managed to break his hold and turned around swiftly to face her attacker and kicked him right between his legs. He let out a yell and staggered out the door in excruciating pain holding his private parts and never tried that again. But after that incident, he verbally abused her every opportunity that presented itself. Her foster mother was a victim of the abuse as well and most of the time seemed oblivious to his degrading attacks on Teresa.

Teresa moved out on her eighteenth birthday. She managed to get a job after school and in two months she had saved up enough money to get a room in a boarding house across town, near her high school. That is where she first saw Ricky Clay, the most popular guy in school. He was handsome, athletic and a real ladies' man. She noticed he smiled at her once, but she never gave it much thought since she was not very popular. Besides, she figured it was her last year in school and would probably never see him again. Little did she know, that ten years later, he would come to work at Paradise, where he would turn her world upside down.

Troy, reflecting on the pain he saw in Teresa's eyes, turned his attention back to Ms. King and asked, "Did you know the grandmother who raised her?"

"No, I never knew her family. She didn't really talk about them much. She said she really did not have any family, so I never pushed. I could see some deep emotional scars that would surface sometimes, but she would quickly change the subject or avoid whatever it was. I always thought it was the pain of being abandoned by her mother when she was ten years old as well as her fiancée when she gave birth to Jamie. He did not want any children and walked out on her for another woman. She was devastated. And now this!! She was head over heels about Ricky and Jamie simply adored him. I personally never did feel good about him."

Troy quickly glanced at his watch. "Well I got enough information and I think I may be able to at least get her out on bail. From all that I have gathered I just need to convince the judge and jury if there is a trial, that she was an innocent victim who was manipulated by a real skilled con man."

"Do you think there will be a trial?" she asked.

"Well, we will know better tomorrow morning when she has to go before the judge. You will be there right?" Troy inquired.

"Yes, yes of course. I will put Jamie on the bus and head out to court," she replied.

"Yes, that will be good. She will need all the support she can get. She is truly traumatized by this whole ordeal and is worried about what will happen to her and Jamie."

"Yes, Troy I know, but I have faith in God. He will work it all out for her and she will be victorious in this ordeal. God already told me," she said, smiling and nodding her head in a matter-of-fact way.

Troy smiled and somehow he knew Ms. King was right. Her words were so reassuring. He rose from his chair and headed toward the door.

"Okay, well I will see you tomorrow morning. Have a good night, Ms. King and thanks so much for the tea." He gave her a warm hug and left.

CHAPTER 51

Monday morning was like most mornings. The sun was shining brightly with the sound of birds chirping, and the honking of the cars and buses adding to the melodious sound of a city coming to life. But this day and morning would be intense. Many lives would be changed and altered; some knowingly and some unknowingly.

Chief Lee finished his cup of coffee on the balcony of his modest two story condominium and quickly drove to the hotel to inform Nate and Lola that Ricky had been arrested. Nate and Lola gave a sigh of relief and quickly gathered their things and checked out of the hotel. Nate told Chief Lee, "I will call you later," (purposely wanting to conceal the gruesome details from Lola). He loved her so much and did not want her to worry about anything. Chief Lee decided not to inform him that Teresa had been arrested as well. He would wait and tell him when he called.

Nate accompanied Lola to the hospital to get her car. He made sure she was safe and settled in at home before leaving to go to work. It was his first day back to Paradise Pillows and fear and trepidation tried to grip the very essence of his soul. A cold chill ran through his body thinking of the confrontation he had with Ricky. "No!" he screamed out loud. *"God has not given me the spirit of fear, but of power and of love and of a sound mind."* He was so grateful to have his life back. He felt like it was a new beginning somehow and was adamant that the devil was not going to bring his spirit down. "God was definitely on my side then, and is on my side now. I will give no place for the devil to disturb my peace," Nate declared. He arrived a few minutes before 8 AM and sat in his car for a while to give thanks to God again. He must now go and unlock the warehouse. "If Ricky were here, the doors would have already been opened and there would be lots of activity going on in the warehouse," he thought, suddenly feeling sad, betrayed and then angry again. He quickly dismissed the thought and said to himself, "Oh well, I thank God I still have Teresa and Sal to help me with the business. They should be here shortly and we can discuss our next move and the future of Paradise Pillows."

He walked over to the main office and unlocked the door. He was so pleased that Teresa had locked his office and held everything together while much chaos was going on when he was hospitalized. All the reports were piled neatly on his desk as if she expected him to return. He smiled at her faith. After going over the inventory report, he was very pleased that the production of Paradise Pillows had not been affected by his absence. "Teresa did an outstanding job, and she is definitely worthy of a nice bonus," he thought, as he made a note on his memo pad to recognize her for all of her hard work.

Engrossed in his work, Nate did not hear Sal come in.

"'Good morning Mr. Bishop. Nice to see you."

Nate was startled by his presence. "Oh, good to see you too, Sal," standing to extend a handshake.

"Is Ricky or Teresa in yet?" he asked, shaking Nate's hand.

"No Ricky is not here, but I am expecting Teresa any minute now. She appears to be running a little late this morning. She is usually here before me," Nate replied.

"So will Ricky be in later?" Sal inquired.

"No, he no longer works here."

Sal frowned as though he did not understand. "What? No disrespect Mr. Bishop, but may I ask why?"

"I will discuss it with you when Teresa gets here and please... call me Nate," he said smiling. "I also wanted to say, I appreciate all of your hard work and would like to talk with you about the possibility of you taking on Ricky's job, with a pay increase of course. If you are willing to give it a shot." Sal was shocked and his facial expression clearly showed it." Look at God!" he thought.

"Oh yes, sure. Thanks Mr. B- - uh, Nate. I really appreciate the opportunity!"

"Also," Sal said changing the subject, "I stopped by here on Saturday to check in with Ricky and this place was swarming with unmarked police cars all over the place. I was taken to the police station where I was held for two hours. They asked me many questions and I was told not to mention the interrogation to anyone."

"Really?" Nate said, "What did you tell them?"

"Nothing, because I did not know anything, except that I work for Paradise Pillows and was hired by Ricky to deliver pillows and pillowcases to the various designated hubs up and down the east coast."

"Oh, I am so sorry that happened to you," Nate said. "This reminds me, I have to make a very important phone call. I will call you back in my office in a few minutes. Okay?"

"Sure, I will be waiting in Ricky's office if that is okay. "

"Actually, I would prefer you wait at Teresa's station." (Nate wanted to make sure everything was left just as it was in case the police needed to investigate Ricky's office). "It should only be a few minutes."

Nate remembered he was supposed to call Chief Lee. "Yes, I am sure he can answer what was going on," he anticipated.

"Hello, Chief Lee, it's Nate Bishop."

"Yes, Nate. I was expecting your call. We made a bust over the weekend which had been under investigation for over a year. It included two of your employees, Ricky Clay and Teresa Hayward."

Nate's heart dropped in disbelief and it began pounding so loudly he could hardly hear.

"Teresa? Teresa Hayward was arrested too? For what?" his voice escalating.

"Apparently her boyfriend, Ricky Clay, kidnapped her and her son and left them in the old shack on the outskirts of town. He confessed. She and her son were able to escape and were found walking along the interstate."

"So why is she in jail?" Nate interrupted somewhat relieved.

"She is being held for aiding and abetting Ricky's drug smuggling. There is enough evidence to hold her. She must go before the judge first this morning."

"Ooh no!! She is not that kind of a girl. She was kidnapped and is now being held for assisting her kidnapper? This makes no sense! This is a mistake! Okay, I know you have to do your job, Chief, but this is a mistake! I am on my way to the courthouse to see what I can do to help her. Thanks so much Chief Lee. Forgive me and please don't take this personally."

"No problem. No problem at all Nate. I understand."

"Oh, by the way, Did you find anything on anyone else who works here? Sal Tully in particular?" Nate asked.

"No, he is as clean as a whistle, not even a parking violation. We interrogated him also on Saturday. We brought him in for questioning. We had no evidence to hold him."

"Okay, thanks again Chief Lee. I gotta run to check on Teresa," as he took notice of the time which was almost 8:30 AM. "Great, I can be there in about fifteen minutes," he thought.

"Sal! Sal!" he yelled.

"Yes, Nate," running quickly upon hearing the anxiety in Nate's voice.

"I have an emergency and I need you to stay here and keep things running. Keep an eye on the guys at the warehouse and I should be back real soon," he said. And just like that...he was gone, leaving Sal with his mouth open and full of more questions than he had answers.

"What is going on? Where is Teresa? Why is Ricky no longer working here?" he wondered.

CHAPTER 52

The courtroom was filled when Nate Bishop arrived. There were many awaiting their fate and others there for moral support. The low rumble of voices began to subside when the bailiff entered the room. Without hesitation he announced, "All rise for the Honorable Les Harris presiding." Judge Harris took his seat and peered out over his courtroom, quickly assessing the crowd, thinking, "Oh dear, this is going to be a long day."

He noticed Nate Bishop in the back of his courtroom and Pastor Sherman too. "It is not unusual to see Pastor Sherman, but why is Nate Bishop here? (hmmm, I thought I just heard he suffered a major stroke and was paralyzed). And who is this very attractive woman?" he asked himself. Ms. King's presence stood out. She had a demeanor about her that was regal and very classy. She always looked strikingly beautiful and poised which was totally opposite of those who were led into the courtroom in shackles, handcuffs and orange jumpsuits.

Judge Harris motioned to the bailiff to come to him. He whispered to the bailiff, "Find out who that lady is and why she is here in my courtroom."

Troy Kennedy was seated in the section with the other attorneys waiting for the name of their clients to be called. Some attorneys came out of their designated area to speak to their clients one on one.

The first person who was led out by two courtroom officers was none other than McKenzie Moore AKA Big Mc. He quietly took a seat near the far end of the courtroom intended for those waiting to see the judge. He looked old and worn. His walk was the walk of defeat which seemed all the more hopeless with the shackles on his ankles and handcuffs on his wrists. He knew his running days had run out. All he could do now was pray and ask God for mercy. He instantly felt God had answered his prayers when he saw Pastor Sherman sitting in the back. A slight head nod between the two were exchanged. "Uhmmm," thought Big Mc, "Why is he here today? Did God tell him I was here?" Somehow, just knowing Pastor Sherman was there gave him hope that maybe it would not be as bad as he thought. "After all, Pastor Sherman has always told me, 'God is a God of Mercy and Grace' and that is something I could definitely use now. Well, I am going to at least be hopeful," he thought.

The bailiff approached Judge Harris and whispered in his ear. "Her name is Joni King and is a mother figure to Teresa Hayward who was arrested over the weekend." He gave a nod to the bailiff and settled back in his oversized chair. The bailiff went out of the courtroom for a few minutes only to arrive with the remainder of those who were arrested over the weekend.

Dante and Billy were brought out together by two officers and were seated in the second row behind Big Mc. They were not allowed to speak to each other, but head nods and eye contacts were evident. Ricky Clay was escorted out last and was able to take the first seat in the second row near the aisle. The six women arrested over the weekend were brought in shackled and handcuffed from the opposite side of the courtroom, and took up the first row of chairs opposite the men. The bailiff was given orders to bring Teresa in without handcuffs and shackles because the evidence was insufficient.

Ricky had already confessed to the police that she was innocent. Chief Lee had spoken to Judge Harris also of her innocence and arranged to have her released after a good verbal thrashing. Teresa did not know of her fate and suddenly forgot everything at the sight of Ricky. Like a flash of lightening, Teresa flew across the room, and taking precise aim at Ricky's head and landed a perfect open handed slap across his face, knocking him out of the chair and onto the floor. Ricky laid in a fetal position bound by the handcuffs and shackles, dazed at the unexpected blunt force to his head. Teresa fell on top of him slapping him repeatedly before the bailiff could pull her off. Teresa screamed, "This is for the hell you have put me through. I trusted you and you did this to me and my son, you low down dirty dog!! You better be glad I am a lady or I would have a few more choice words for you!" She was still kicking and screaming as the bailiff handcuffed her and removed her from the courtroom. Everyone in the courtroom was on their feet trying to see what was happening. Some were cheering her on.

Judge Harris stood pounding his gavel and shouting, "There will be order in my courtroom!! Sit down!! Order in the room...Order!!" His anger and outrage were very noticeable. In a matter of seconds, there was an overflow of officers in place bringing order to the courtroom. Several guards immediately surrounded the suspects and made sure they were secure. One officer made a quick assessment of Ricky's injuries and treated him for a nose bleed and a lump on his head which was sustained when he fell.

Troy Kennedy immediately left the courtroom to find Teresa. He was really worried now. He had a really good argument and felt confident that he would be able to get her out with bail, and perhaps have it totally dismissed for lack of evidence. But now after this outburst he wondered if there would be additional charges of assault and battery. Ms. King tried to run to Teresa but was ordered back to her seat or be escorted out of the courtroom. *"Oh, God, Please help us all!"* she cried. *"What can I do Lord? Please, what should I do?"* Tears rolling down her face, she heard a small voice say. *"Be still and know that I am God."* This calmed Ms. King's spirit and she sat once again very regal and refined, eager to see what would happen next. "God will make a way somehow," she declared. *"Thank you Jesus. I trust you."*

It was a bittersweet moment for Billy and Dante. They were happy and relieved to see Ricky and to know he did not betray them and run off with the money. Seeing him in jail with them explained everything except where the money was. Being true and loyal to each other was good, but none of that mattered at the moment. They all could be going away behind prison walls for a long, long time. They both had faith in Ricky and believed that if they ever got out of prison, they were confident Ricky had hidden the three and a half million dollars someplace safe.

Big Mc was extremely worried now that Teresa's attack on Ricky had angered the judge. "Uhmph, I am already in big trouble and at the court's mercy and now I have to stand before an angry judge." Fearful of his fate, Big Mc muttered a prayer under his breath, *"God please be merciful to me. I know I don't deserve it but please help me."*

The courtroom stenographer entered the court with many files and placed them on the judge's desk. After a brief conversation, she took her seat and the bailiff called the court to order. The first name called were Billy's and then Dante's to stand before the judge. Judge Harris quickly skimmed their files and called the bailiff and court stenographer to approach his bench. "These guys belong to the Feds based on the Racketeer Influenced and Corrupt Organizations (RICO) Act Law of 1970. They will be extradited to Federal Court this afternoon in White Plains, New York. The Feds are on their way here now. Take them back to their jail cells. McKenzie Moore and Ricky

Clay are to go as well. They are all part of this criminal enterprise of racketeering, drug sales, bribery, blackmail, extortion and kidnapping. But, I must address Ricky Clay before you take him. Ricky Clay will you approach my bench."

Judge Harris looked squarely at him and said, "Ricky Clay in all fairness to the law which I uphold, I witnessed you being physically assaulted in my courtroom. Do you wish to press charges against the lady who attacked you?"

"No, your honor. I actually deserved it," he replied. Those who witnessed the incident giggled loudly, again irritating Judge Harris. He slammed his gavel down again. "Order in this room! Take your seat Mr. Clay." As Ricky turned to go back to his seat, he quickly scanned the audience and locked eyes with Nate Bishop. "Did the slap affect my mind and am I now hallucinating? Nate was in the hospital dying and completely paralyzed. How could this be?" he thought to himself. Blinking his eyes and unable to rub them because of the handcuffs, he tried to refocus. He was in shock and stood still, frozen in disbelief. Nate could not help himself. He flashed a big smile and winked at Ricky.

"Take your seat Ricky Clay, NOW!" Judge Harris's deep baritone voice added to Ricky's astonishment causing him to jump. Trying to recover, Ricky quickly walked toward his seat without breaking his stare with Nate and stumbled, landing into the chair awkwardly. Again, more snickering and laughter filled the courtroom.

Judge Harris yelled, "Get this clown out of my courtroom!" pounding his gavel again.

The bailiff took him to join the rest of those waiting for the Federal Agents to get there. He paused and whispered to the judge, "Your Honor, what about the woman, Teresa Hayward? Shall I take her back to her jail cell as well?"

"No," Judge Harris said, "No. Put her in the temporary holding cell. I want to give her some time to think about her actions and I will call for her later."

"Yes, Your Honor," he replied.

The temporary holding cell was right outside the main courtroom intended for the very aggressive suspects who become belligerent or confrontational in court.

CHAPTER 53

Troy Kennedy sprinted through the door following the bailiff who had subdued Teresa. The bailiff encouraged Troy to join them in the hope of helping to calm her down. He opened the holding cell and motioned for her to go in. Troy joined her. Before locking the cell, the bailiff told Troy to yell when he was ready to come out. Troy nodded his head and took a seat next to Teresa on the hard wooden bench. Touching her lightly on her shoulder, he said, "Boy, you are one feisty lady. I must admit that was the first open-handed knock out slap I have ever witnessed." He smiled not sure how she was going to react. Teresa, turned slowly to the sound of his voice next to her. She did not notice Troy was locked in the cell with her. She was confused. "What did you just say?" Troy repeated exactly what he had said, "Boy, you are one feisty lady. I must admit that was the first open-handed knock out slap I have ever witnessed."

"Yep that is what I thought you said," as she burst out laughing. "He deserved it and so much more!" Troy agreed and soon they both were laughing out of control. His method of calming her worked!

Troy was an excellent judge of character. He had learned so much about her the past two days. He had spent the remainder of the day with her on Saturday, after her arrest and then all day on Sunday. They talked about many things. He promised her he was going to redeem her and now he was very worried that she may be held for assault, battery and possibly contempt of court because many people witnessed the attack. "I feel something very special in my heart for her and I will redeem her at all cost. I know she is innocent and I will prove it. She is an amazingly beautiful woman," he thought, "Even when she is angry," making a mental note to watch out for the knock-out slap if he ever angered her. He chuckled to himself.

Three hours passed and Judge Harris finally called for a recess at 11:30 AM. The day was totally chaotic. It seemed every person who stood before him to meet their fate had body language which was very disrespectful. They muttered under their breath, sucked their teeth, rolled their eyes, and were just short of contempt. He had had enough and needed a break. "I knew it was going to be one of those days," he said. "It seems Teresa Hayward's disrespectful energy is still lingering in my courtroom. I will see her after lunch!"

"Court will reconvene again at 12:45," he declared, pushing himself away from his desk.

Nate Bishop and Pastor Sherman headed immediately to join Ms. King. Nate was happy to see her again as he reflected on her powerful prayer and faith in Jesus Who healed him completely and filled him with the Holy Spirit. Pastor Sherman was happy to see her too, because he understood the power of prayer and the power of agreement with another believer. Ms. King quickly introduced Nate to her pastor and suggested they go outside to talk and pray. Each of them witnessed Teresa's attack on Ricky and were very concerned that she may have made the situation worse. They had not been able to see her or her attorney since she was physically removed from the courtroom. Pastor Sherman's car was the closest, so they decided to sit in his car and pray. They each took turns and prayed and believed God for Teresa to be released until it was time for court to resume. They entered the court and sat together this time.

The bailiff announced again, "All rise, the Honorable Les Harris, presiding." Everyone rose and Judge Harris took his seat along with the courtroom stenographer. Judge Harris beckoned the bailiff to bring in

Teresa Hayward. He quickly returned with her and Troy. Troy stepped up to the bench to address the judge.

"Your Honor, on behalf of my client, Teresa Hayward, she is humbly apologetic for her outburst in your court and asks for your forgiveness."

Judge Harris said, "Have your client approach the bench. I wish to speak to her directly." Teresa was no longer laughing, but visibly shaking. Grateful that she was able to make it across the courtroom, she unconsciously slipped her arm in Troy's arm to steady herself. Troy pretended not to notice as tears rolled down her face.

"Teresa Hayward, you showed me personally today, that you lack self control and actually attacked a man in my courtroom causing bodily harm. That in itself is a misdemeanor with severe penalties in the criminal justice system and if convicted this could mean jail time or probation or even mandatory anger management classes, as well as a fine. You are in serious trouble young lady! And now you stand before me having been arrested for aiding and abetting a drug dealer who was smuggling drugs along the east coast. Under the RICO Act of 1970, committing any action that assists in the crime, can have you charged just as the person who actually committed the crime. If found guilty you could be facing twenty years to life in prison. Are you aware of that young lady?" Teresa's trembling legs buckled and for the first time she realized she was holding onto Troy's arm which kept her standing upright. The thought of being incarcerated for all those years away from Jamie was something she simply could not fathom.

"How do you plead?"

Troy spoke up quickly, "Not guilty, Your Honor, and if this should go to trial, I am prepared to prove beyond a reasonable doubt that my client was manipulated and taken advantage of. She had no knowledge of assisting in drug trafficking."

Judge Harris seemed to have dismissed Troy's plea on her behalf and continued to address Teresa.

"Ms. Hayward, you must have a special relationship with your Creator and have made a great impression on many people in this community whom I highly respect. Many have spoken to me about you and your character. Some of those same people also fell victim to this same master manipulator. That tells me you are a trusting individual who was befriended by a blatant narcissistic criminal who, if found guilty, could be put away for a long time. Nevertheless, because of your outburst in my courtroom, I am going to give you a conditional discharge. This means, as long you are a model citizen with no encounters with the police for the next six months, then all your records will be expunged. Be sure to see the court clerk to make an appointment to follow up with me in six months. You are released and case dismissed!"

Teresa let go of Troy's arm and bowed down giving homage to God and then to Judge Harris as she wept softly. Troy and Judge Harris gave her a moment to recover. Troy gently reached down and helped her to her feet to escort her out of the courtroom. Nate Bishop, Pastor Sherman, and Ms. King, trying hard to suppress their shouts of praise, (as court was still in session), joined them as they left the courtroom.

Judge Harris hammered his gavel and said, "Next case is...." and the door closed. Teresa heard the sound of the door close with a heavy thud which seemed to solidify her past. "It is closed forever! It is the end of this bizarre nightmare," she thought. She quickly reflected on the fact that even though it was painful, if all of those events did not occur, she would not have experienced God's Love and His Saving Grace.

Eternally grateful for everyone's love and support, she cried tears of joy as she hugged everyone. Pastor Sherman gave Teresa a hug and asked everyone to hold hands as they prayed and gave thanks to God for yet another miracle.

"And we know Father God," said Pastor Sherman, *"that sometimes **The Plan, The Thought and The Purpose** You have for us can be painful and lead us in many unknown directions, but yet we know and are fully persuaded that all things are working together for good to them that love You Father God... And so we continue to trust and praise You through it all. It is You Father and You alone who are faithful, kind, and true. It is You Father who knows the plan and thoughts that You think toward us, thoughts of peace and not of evil to give us hope and a future (paraphrased Jeremiah 29:11). May we always worship You in Spirit and in Truth. Thank You Father. In Jesus Name. Amen!!"*

Dear Reader:

Thank you so much for taking the time to read this novel. I hope you enjoyed it and I would love to know your thoughts, so please make your comments on my web page...

www.planthoughtpurpose.com

or my social media Facebook page, Carrie E. Robinson.

If you would like to contact me for your personalized copy, please email me @ CRobinson420@yahoo.com.

If you would like to share this book with friends as a gift for any and all occasions, go to our secured website and place your orders @

https://www.paypal.com/cgi-bin/webscr?cmd=_s-xclick&hosted_button_id=ECUQVKU8JP6C6

Thanks again and as always... You are important to God and are greatly loved. Your existence has purpose! Wise men seek him. Continued blessings!!!

Made in the USA
Middletown, DE
16 November 2014